Baltimore Beauties and Beyond
Volume Two

 C&T PUBLISHING

Baltimore Beauties

and Beyond

Studies in

Classic Album Quilt Appliqué

Volume Two

by Elly Sienkiewicz

Published by
C & T Publishing
P.O. Box 1456
Lafayette, California 94549

Library of Congress Cataloging-in-Publication Data
(Revised for volume 2)

Sienkiewicz, Elly
   Baltimore beauties and beyond.

   Includes bibliographical references.
   1. Appliqué—Patterns.   2. Album quilts—Maryland—
Baltimore.   3. Patchwork—Patterns.   I. Title.
TT779.S54   1989   746.9′7   89-60479
   ISBN   0-914881-23-X (v. 1)
   ISBN   0-914881-40-X (hardcover : v. 2)
   ISBN   0-914881-34-5 (softcover : v. 2)

Title Page Calligraphy by Walter J. Filling
Frontispiece: Album Quilt, mid-nineteenth century. Gift of Mrs. George Stonehill,
Brooklyn Museum of Art, Brooklyn, New York. Photo courtesy of the Brooklyn Museum of Art.
Front Cover Photo:
Detail: signed *Margaret D. Meredith*, from a quilt inscribed, in part, *Baltimore* and *1847*. (Photo 4-34).
From the collection of the Lovely Lane Museum, United Methodist Historical Society, Baltimore, Maryland.
Photo courtesy of The Baltimore Museum of Art.
Photography by Sharon Risedorph, San Francisco,
and through the courtesy of the contributors as noted.

Edited by Sayre Van Young, Berkeley, California
Illustrations by Julie Olson, Washington, D.C., and Randy Miyake/Miyake Illustration
Composition/Production Coordination by Publishers Design Studio, Mill Valley, California

First Edition
First Printing
Printed in the United States of America

Contents

The Color Section begins after Page 80

Acknowledgments

My grateful thanks to C & T Publishing, for their faith in this book and for being such a pleasant and honorable team to work with, and to those who have helped so much with this book: Julie Olson, Laurel Horton, and Lesley Arietti.

A special thank you to Sayre Van Young, for her skilled and patient editing, and to Kathy Mannix, who allayed the stress of repeated deadlines with her easy charm and intelligent assistance. Also, my thanks to Mary Sue Hannan, for aiding business on the home front. Thank you to Walter J. Filling for the generous gift of calligraphy for the title page and for the chapter on Victorian inkings.

And thank you to my college friend, now quilt friend, Margaret Kaufman, for the poems which enrich this book. I appreciate so much as well all those who have contributed both the needlework and the photographs which grace these pages.

Many have been kind and helpful with the underlying research for this series and I would particularly like to thank Stephen Patrick, Curator, George Washington Memorial Masonic Temple in Alexandria, Virginia; S. Brent Morris, Book Review Editor of *The Scottish Rite Journal*; Barbara Franco, Curator of the Museum of Our National Heritage in Lexington, Massachusetts; Reverend Edwin Schell of the United Methodist Historical Society; and Eva Sleazak of the Enoch Pratt Free Library in Baltimore. All have been helpful in trying to sleuth out some of the fraternal symbols and buildings reflected in these classic quilts. Especial thanks and appreciation to the Needleartists, the Latter-day Good Ladies of Baltimore, both those whose gifts of time and talent have already enriched the *Baltimore Beauties* series and those whose art is yet to grace the volumes to come.

Thank you once again to my mother, Eileen Mary Clare-Patton Hamilton-Wigner, for all that a mother is, and to my siblings David and Erica for caring to keep family close. And thank you, my children, Donald, Alex, and Katya. That you are still with us much of the time, to warm and lighten our hearts, is a great joy. Thank you Stan, mate and helpmeet, for walking all these extra miles.

This book is dedicated to my
husband, my most plainspoken critic,
and most cherished friend.

Author's Preface

Might midcentury look to the future as well as the past, while end-century looks back more tenaciously on what has been? When I was a schoolgirl mid-twentieth century, George Orwell's just-published *1984* seemed so terribly modern in its fictional predictions, and that future seemed so far away. But 1984 came and went with things both more worrisome and more wondrous than even Orwell conjured. And now here we are, close up against the end of the twentieth century. And while my younger years marveled at the technology and futurism of the movie, *2001: A Space Odyssey*, my middle years have been a time of holding close that which I have, a time of learning where I've come from, and yes, a time of making quilts, heirlooms, to record and work some magic in my sojourn on this earth.

Perhaps it is simply my middle years, but one senses a mood at the end of the century. It echoes something of the end of the nineteenth century: a pervasive spirit of celebration, a review of accomplishment. The beginning of the final decade of the century provides a time where, for posterity, we can look not at the problems unsolved, but at the sweep of history. In the manner of all celebrations, we can choose to focus on the good that has come, on the real accomplishments, on that of which we can be proud. We may never be able to salvage the unspoiled enthusiasm which dubbed an epoch "The Age of Progress," but surely we have much to rejoice over, much to be grateful for. For we, too, have lived in momentous times.

The mood of the last decades of the twentieth century seems to have a large element of conserving, of looking backward for guidance as well as of preparing for the future. This seems to be part of the appeal of antiques in general and of the classic Baltimore-style Album Quilts in particular. For the makers of the Album Quilts seem to have sought through these quilts to commemorate, or to witness religious faith or patriotism, or to express thanks and appreciation, or to remember or be remembered, or something of each. They suit our frame of mind, as we ponder the past, the present, and the future in the last decade of the twentieth century. For quilts are fragile threads in time tying us to each other, to those who have come before and to those who will come after. They are magical threads, appropriately cherished.

You and I are quiltmakers ourselves. We aspire to make Albums, works of beauty, and seemingly we make them for much the same and diverse reasons as those whose needlepath we follow. For my part, I believe our quilts will wrap those we love and those we leave behind in warmth, sharing with them a taste of our hopes and dreams. Our quilts weave a song to sit on the shoulder of the future, to whisper in the ear of the sewer, or to crescendo at exhibition, or simply to comfort, almost inaudibly, a background melody from the ancestral chest. For old quilts, like old friends, tie people to their past, offer comfort to their present, and nurture hope for the future. So come, my friends. On to our own heirloom Albums, and "Au fin du siécle!" To the end of the century!

Elly Sienkiewicz
Eleanor Patton Hamilton Sienkiewicz
Washington, D.C.
January 6, 1990

Old Quilts

You come upon them sometimes
folded away into trunks lined with paper,
fragile and dry as blue hydrangea,
or you find them stuffed in a wad
at the base of a wardrobe, old quilts,
color reduced to an idea, stained
with love or death,
nothing that can be rubbed away.

They appear as interstitial tissue
linking us to someone else's labor.
Sometimes, whole pieces fall away
no matter how carefully you take them up —
they shred into nothing, leaving thin ribbons,
a ribbon, a space, a nothing,
as if, in serious conversation, the other
falls silent, leaves it up to you.

And you could, in a dark mood, say
that's all any of it comes to,
shreds, fluff, fragments,
but that is not the mood that connects,
not what makes you spread the quilts to light
when you find them cast away.

You hesitate before brooming spiders' webs,
you save old letters, pin up children's crayon
drawings, lay out the best silver every day.
Beauty lies not only in the making of a thing
but in its use, not in its preservation
but in its wearing down.

Margaret Fleischer Kaufman

Introduction

Thank you for joining me as we continue our journey to bygone Baltimore and beyond. Rather than diminishing, interest in mid-nineteenth-century Maryland's Album Quilts seems to have grown apace in the time since we began our journey together in *Volume I* of *Baltimore Beauties*. Through the interval, these quilts' myriad, yet repetitious block shapes, fabrics, and colors stayed in my memory and sent me off to study increasing numbers of Album Quilts and related archival materials.

The incredible wealth of these appliquéd Albums makes it clear that for those Maryland quiltmakers, this was not just a hobby, it was an involvement. Moreover, this involvement was widespread and abiding. No major definitive evidence about authorship has been unearthed, but incrementally, clues to enlighten us about these women's quilt-making passion are accumulating. Enough design evidence and written evidence exists to appreciate a pervading spirit and warmth of feeling about these quilts. There are no conclusive answers to much of the mystery concerning who made them and why, and yet the appreciation of them grows greater and greater. And surely this, after all, must be some measure of how good art affects us.

At this point in our journey together, we need to consider the presentation of that quilt which has been evolving both in our imagination and in fact. *Volume II* treats, above all, the completed Albums, whereas *Volume I* and its pattern companion (*Baltimore Album Quilts — Historic Notes and Antique Patterns*) concentrated on blocks alone. Thus Chapter 5 discusses sets and borders, quilting and binding. And something of the design scope and possibilities of the Album Quilt genre is presented in Chapter 4's Quilt Gallery, a collection of quilt photos, which continues in the Color Section. We'll visit with all manner of Album Quilt presentations there and focus our taste so that our own quilts can be taken even more beautifully "beyond" Baltimore. Patterns for twenty blocks and thirteen borders are included in "Part Three: The Patterns," with the promise of more borders to come in this volume's pattern companion.

The theme of "The Album" seems increasingly to focus and imbue our own growing familiarity with the classic Baltimore Album Quilts. It makes them more understandable, not in an easy way where the answers are all laid out and writ clear, but as albums, "collections on a theme," have always informed us: broadly, elusively, incompletely, and yet with such vivid specifics that we are better able to conceive the dimensions of the subject they reflect. Memory albums, whether of cloth or paper, flowers or photographs, seem above all to be connectors. They connect a bride to the friends and family of her youth, a group to an honored member or leader, and patriots to each other and to shared history. And what of Friendship Albums? Was it, as some have written, "the romanticization and sentimentalization of friendship"? Perhaps that assessment is a bit harsh. For surely the women who gave beautiful hand-wrought blocks, sweetly inscribed, would also offer succor and support to a friend in need? We are richer, today, for their open and outspoken valuing of friendship, their reminder to cherish each other, friend, family, and compatriot alike.

Appropriately, the concept of "The Album" has furnished, as well, the theme which unites the *Baltimore Beauties* series. For, much like a detective story where first one lead, then another, is pursued, some of the series has been written as articles, some even pre-published, each looking at a given aspect of these quilts in detail. One such is Chapter 6, "Dr. Dunton, Mary Evans, and the Baltimore Album Quilt Attributions," which treats a subject first addressed in *Volume I*. Another issue, one seemingly unique to these quilts, is that of picture blocks. And thus Chapter 3 presents how to make those blocks which serve as portraits in fabric of people, places, and memorable things. Like a conversation among friends with shared enthusiasms, interests, and acquaintances, the chapters in these volumes range widely, and share information, techniques, and possible insights into these old quilts. As in a conversation among friends, there is no pretense of infallability, nor final answers, and little summation or recapping. But the sum of these voices in conversation helps to tell a story, the story of the classic Baltimore Album Quilts and the women who made them. And above the din of incredible complexity of graphic images, needlework styles, and subject themes, the strong bright thread which unites all those antique Album Quilts and ours to them, can be seen and understood. This thread weaves the Album themes, "to remember" and "to be remembered."

How to Use This Book

With the informality of those who journey together, the assumption is made that you have read *Volume I* and have it as a nearby reference. Thus little from that volume is repeated here. *Baltimore Beauties and Beyond: Studies in Classic Album Quilt Appliqué — Volume II,* presents twenty blocks and thirteen border patterns. Pattern notes for the block patterns refer to lessons from *Volume I* and give pertinent background information.

A full-color photo of each pattern's block will help you select your appliqué fabric. "Part One: Getting Started" in *Volume I* provides important information on how to transfer the patterns (given here on one, two, and four pages) from the book to make your own complete 12½" finished-size pattern. Borders are presented from half of the symmetrical border corner motif to at least half of the first running border motif. To use, trace the border

design onto freezer paper and repeat the number of motif units needed for the size border appropriate to your quilt.

Fifty quilts are exhibited in this volume: forty-five antique and five contemporary. Throughout this book, when a quilt is referred to by number (as quilt #1, or quilt #5), you will find it pictured in the Color Section. The Quilt Gallery (Chapter 4), featuring Photos 4-1 through 4-34, is an extensive collection of black-and-white photos of quilts. If you are wondering about the needleartists who worked on the contemporary quilts and blocks pictured, see "Part Two: The Quiltmakers."

When a specific block is referred to, for example, as "quilt #4, block D-2," that block can be located by its letter and number: the letters refer to the block position in the quilt, reading from left to right, and the numbers refer to position from top to bottom.

Deep in the Territory

Even the trees are different here,
Don't look right, bend toward the river in a foreign way
Like women washing laundry over stones.

Three years since we saw you,
Stopped in this prairie town so far
From home, deep in the Territory.
Still it startles me when Indian women appear —
I never hear them —
They are suddenly quietly there
Leaning into the shade of the house
Against the Kansas glare.

I'm used to calling solitude my friend,
George travelling so far from farm to farm
But it slips through my fingers when the women come.
I confess myself glad to greet them
Though it troubles me the way they walk right in,
As if our house were landscape only.

I can tell they don't admire my tea.
What draws them is the album quilt.
They never take their silent leave
Without standing at our bed, touching it.
They turn it all around, tug the binding.
I stand there watching much like
Women with babies when strangers
Pinch their cheeks, nervous
Yet proud like that, fearful
In the odd, cold way that fear takes hold
When there's no common tongue.

How can I sign "friend" to them,
Explain that Edith stitched those wreaths,
Evaline, the goose tracks pointing out?
As if it were yesterday
I see us working at the frame
In the church hall Wednesday nights.
Though it puzzles them, I chant your names
To the Indian women: "Edith," I whisper,
"Evaline, Mary Lou."

Margaret Fleischer Kaufman

Part One: The Chapters

June 1990

Laura B. Anthony · Washington, D.C.

Chapter One

The Album

Who among us has not collected? Vignettes of gathering and ordering go back to my earliest childhood. Snapshots of picking privet berries to fill dimpled fists and seeking stones for snowsuit pockets picture me, acquisitive, as a toddler. They bring a smile to mind, thinking back on my own children's myriad and passing collections. Into their lives, as into mine, came the albums — photo albums, stamp collections, scrapbooks, and memory books. Some albums were heirloom precious: my father's young family photograph album, and his World War II M.I.T. Radiation Laboratory record album now recalling the classic age of American physics. Later, seeing my interest in such things, my great Aunt Elsie Crowley gave me an Album Quilt. Inscribed, in part, "Mrs. Eliza Palmer," and "1854," it had come to her through her New York State ancestors. A collection of separately signed, same-shaped appliqués, it appears to be a friendship Album Quilt, made of different red calicoes. Surely those same collecting passions that seem forever to have bound quiltmakers — avid assemblers of fabric, patterns, and threaded technologies — inform the classic Album quilts.

Album Quilts, like their book-made counterparts, house collections on a theme. The making of both types of albums swelled to fad-like status in the middle decades of the nineteenth century. Study of each leads to understanding of the other, creation of both being a cultural phenomenon of significant proportions. Album Quilts seem to have been made up the coastal states and into Ohio, Tennessee, and Indiana, at least. But while Album Quilts occurred broadly, it seems to be the Baltimore Album Quilts, a rather loosely defined term, that are distinguished by their particular attributes, beauty, and great numbers. While the aesthetic characteristics of the genre are the subject of the whole *Baltimore Beauties* series, the question of why the genre was so astonishingly popular, and particularly so in the vicinity of Baltimore, Maryland, is the focus of this chapter.

Twentieth-century quilt scholars have enjoyed both recounting and speculating upon possible Album Quilt themes. The hypothetical roll call of mid-nineteenth-century Album Quilts echoes like a syllabus from an American cultural history course: Legacy quilts, Sampler quilts, Freedom quilts, Bride's quilts, Tithing quilts, Retirement quilts, Presentation Albums, Friendship quilts, Friendship Medley Albums, Autograph Albums, Family Autograph Albums, Family Record Albums, Death-watch quilts, Scripture quilts, Bible quilts, and Quotation quilts. A visitor to bygone Baltimore might suggest adding Memorial Albums, Patriotic Albums, History Albums, Botanical Albums, Natural History Albums, Missionary Albums, Fraternal Order Albums, even Political Sentiment Albums. But, in truth, many Baltimore-style Album Quilts seem more ornately Victorian, even, in concept than any of these listed, being themselves a collection of blocks on a whole collection of themes. Admittedly, though, part of their fascination today is that their intentions remain obscured. This invites conjecture, but cautions that what we are engaged in is speculation.

Numerous factors seem to account, in combination, for the popularity of the Album Quilt at mid-nineteenth century. Relatively recent technology was important. It had provided commercially available permanent, nonfugitive India ink ("a black pigment of lampblack mixed with a gelatinous substance") and colorfast domestic Turkey red and Victoria green cotton. In addition, the varietal wealth of port city fabrics cannot be underestimated as a stimulus. Elegant imported chintzes, printed floral and geometric stripes for borders and sashings, rainbow prints, and other sophisticated quiltmaking fabrics were at hand for purchase. Then, too, a certain Baltimore "look" was achieved by German zephyr wool imported for Berlin work, but seemingly used by our ladies of Baltimore for flat, straight, and satin-stitch embroidery on Album appliqué. Silk floss was available too, for straight, back, and buttonhole stitching. Surely this material wealth fueled the Album Quilt fashion in Baltimore City. Similarly today, use of a particularly effective print, or easy-to-use permanent pens and a fondness for inkwork, perhaps, spur us on with the pleasure of success. Demography must be credited also. One is struck in studying the Maryland Album Quilts by the concomitant blossoming of some exceptional appliquéd Albums in New York State in particular. Surely the fact that New York and Baltimore were the nation's two largest seaports in this mercantile clipper ship era affected the sophistication reached by some of their quiltmaking citizens. In just such a way, modern quilt guilds, shops, and symposia provide us with inspirational goods, and a heady infusion of technical knowledge.

And what of cultural history in explaining the Album phenomenon? To begin with, Victorian Americans seem, above all, to have cherished human attachments. Baltimore Albums are threaded both literally and symbolically with the concepts of civic caring, patriotism and personal loyalty, benevolence and "Christian virtues," and friendship. Migrations to western territories kept America on the move. In a bustling seaport such as Baltimore, fare-thee-wells must have been commonplace. The desire to make remembrances for friends and family moving away was surely one reason for Album Quilts in the middle decades of the nineteenth century. These quilts would have covered attachments, stitched them finely in, and thus served as comforts to both those leaving and to those being left behind. There seem, though, to have been as many different reasons, as many different levels of emotion, for making these quilts then as we have for making our quilts now. And the form which giving Album blocks might have taken admits of variety, as well. There is ample evidence that "Album Quilts" may have been given in any stage of making, from a collection of blocks (not necessarily a complete set), to finished tops, to, in all likelihood, completed quilts.[1]

There seems to have been many quilts inspired by devoted groups of people. Quilts inscribed to pastors indicate religious groups (including classes), as quiltmaking bodies. Certain Baltimore Album Quilts point to other connections: friends, neighbors, or relatives of someone lost to the Mexican War; communities closing rank in memoriam, people honoring others; or sewers supporting struggling fellow Americans in "Texas!" We suspect quiltmakers of silently expressing the sentiment: statehood — slave or free — or their political passion — Whig or Democrat. Then, too, we may meet friends and family of a bride-to-be, or pupils in a Female Seminary making a quilt for a pastor's departure or a missionary's return. And some quilts hint at fundraising roles, conceivably, for a new fraternal lodge, a Friendly Insurance Society, or a church charity. Overall, and imbuing the very air of bygone Baltimore, is the sense that perhaps some major factor or event, something memorialized from the past, perhaps an anniversary, or something occurring in the present — even something expectantly awaited in the future — had spurred on the making of a good many of those quilts. Who knows but that even a concept (such as "Geometry," which symbolized moral perfection to the Freemasons, or "obligated Odd Fellowship") may have had a pervasive effect on the making of many of these quilts?

Photo 1-1. The Album

But while the genre seems to have been begun and to have continued with considerable group contributions, some Album Quilts seem then to have been designed either by individual quiltmakers or by one person or group overseeing the designing and making of a given quilt. Watching today's quiltmakers, one must entertain the idea that quiltmakers then, as now, made Album Quilts as works of art have always been made, simply to express oneself in a unique creation. Such a quiltmaker might have intended to keep the quilt herself, as a memory album, an heirloom, rather than to present it to someone else. William Rush Dunton, an early twentieth-century Album expert, voiced these same thoughts, writing in *Old Quilts*, "The suspicion occurs to me that there occurred a change in custom as to the making of these album quilts. That originally they were made up of blocks presented and signed by friends, but gradually ladies began to make the blocks themselves, finally making all needed for a quilt and may have asked their friends to sign them."[2] So we seem to have intertwined traditions in the classic Album Quilts: that of the group and that of the individually designed (though possibly group-made) quilt, and quilts made both for presentation and for keeping oneself.

Social mores must have contributed to the wealth, variety, and popularity of the Album Quilt. The "veneration of friendship" was one such and it would have been enriched by women's seminaries where both friendship and handicraft arts flourished. Certainly the autograph album books of the period reveal profuse expressions of friendship inscribed both by seemingly young women to each other and by young men to young women. Such "friendship's offerings" seem often to be interspersed with moral and religious entreaties from parents, siblings, and other overtly devout well-wishers. Some of the surviving autograph albums include dates covering a period of several years, as well as signatures accompanied by town, city, county, and state names that were sometimes quite distant from one another, indicating both the long-term interest in collecting sentiments, and the mobility of the population. With capitalistic creativity, publishers responded to this market with attractively bound albums of blank pages interspersed with scriptural or botanical engravings. Their popularity was nourished by other books containing album passages for cribbing, and elegant Christmas season anthologies called "offerings." Entertaining and morally enriching, two popular ones were *Friendship's Offering* and *The Odd Fellow Offering*. There were also elaborate parlor albums, books both entertaining and decorative. One such, in the Winterthur Museum Manuscript Collection, notes that it was made by one woman for, and at the request of, another. That fine commission piece includes poetry, sermon extracts, sketches, and watercolors of plants and birds.

Another social phenomenon already underway was the "cult of domesticity." While it prevailed, industrious practice of home arts, particularly needlework, had the aspect of moral virtue. Combined with the widely promoted ideal of pursuing "rational pleasures" such as the study of natural history, these mixed domestic and intellectual missions met happily in Album Quilt making. As a genre, in fact, Baltimore Album Quilts comprise virtuoso expressions of history, botany, ornithology, popular needlearts, religion, classicism, calligraphy, and current affairs. Some, of course, seem markedly less ambitious. On the other hand, perhaps we underestimate them, for these quilts seem to speak through a symbolic tongue which we can only faintly hear. But we must remember how openly, even to effusion, Victorians expressed patriotism, moral beliefs, religious convictions, and affection between friends. Such convictions are penned in words onto the Album Quilts, but heartfelt sensibilities are there, too, through symbols, those visible signs of invisible things.

The mid-nineteenth century surely seems to have been the age of associations of all sorts, for social groups were joined in multiples by men and women alike. A man might belong to both the Masons and the Odd Fellows,[3] the militia, one of Baltimore's volunteer fire departments, be a lay leader of a weekly religious class, pursue a career as a lawyer or cannery owner, and head a large family. It seems to have been a phenomenally social time in the life of our nation, and this undoubtedly affected the large amount of social history reflected in the Album Quilts. For example, the Methodist system of primary loyalty to weekly religious classes and Sunday's opportunity to follow a favorite pastor in the circuit ministry expanded one's church circle beyond a narrow congregation. Discovering that many names on classic Baltimore Album Quilts are also on Methodist Church class rolls, one wonders if this enlarged religious circle wasn't a major factor in encouraging the spread of quilt designs, fabric usage, and of friendships. Picture blocks in some Maryland Album Quilts depict churches, missions, or a fraternal lodge. These, as well as presentational inscriptions on other quilts, indicate the crucial connection of organized groups to the flourishing of the Album Quilt genre.

By midcentury, causes abounded. Even the women's rights movement had its origins then; the first conference on the topic met in Seneca Falls, New York, having been convened in 1848 by Elizabeth Cady Stanton and Lucretia Mott. To some degree, the virtues Odd Fellowdom emphasized — kindness, charity, cooperative spirit, and overall benevolence — were considered woman's virtues. Imagine the anticipation, then, when news spread that a new "fraternal" degree, the "obligated Order of the Daughters of Rebekah," was to be established. When, in 1851, the first women's order of the Odd Fellows opened with the Crown Rebekah Lodge on Fels Road, Baltimore, it witnessed officially the already changing status of women. Palpable excitement must have preceded the lodge's opening and stimulated much preparatory activity in homes. And would not quiltmaking almost inevitably focus such quiet jubilation?

Wavelike, America's quilt types reveal hope-filled anticipation of events, from bride's quilts, to centennial quilts, to bicentennial quilts, to the Statue of Liberty centennial quilts. Baltimore's great expectations, though elusive to define, must swell those billows as well. And among all that Odd Fellow iconography in these Baltimore quilts, the coming of the Rebekahs, too, must be so heralded. Meanwhile, wives and daughters of Masons continued to meet in homes until the Order of the Eastern Star became official some twenty-five years later. While Masonic moral tenets and symbolism still permeated the ethos of the Baltimore Album era, public Masonic display, earlier so sumptuously integrated into civic life, was well on the upswing from the restraint precipitated by a scandal setting off anti-Masonic sentiments in the 1830s. But wives and daughters of Masons (many of whom were Odd Fellows also) seem to have sewn their solidarity into these quilts as well.

Changing times may have given new purpose to the tradition of quiltmaking. Already industrialization had taken its toll. The depression of 1839-

1843 had underscored the urban factory worker's vulnerability to unemployment. Aiding the poor, the Victorian "Lady Bountiful's" duty, must have appealed to women as devout, industrious, and benevolent as many of the quiltmakers appear to have been. One wonders if they might not somehow have turned their needles to raise money for charities through church or fraternal affiliations. The increasing prosperity of American society and the growing and servanted middle-class must surely have affected the pursuit of a leisure-time activity such as art quilt making, as well. That an Album Quilt might also be morally didactic, that it might aid charity or otherwise tangibly witness benevolence, and that its representations could glorify nature, "the pencil of God," must have made Album Quilts a fully uplifting, not to mention comforting, pursuit. And this comfort of community connectedness may have been fundamental to the Album Quilts.

For yes, these times were a-changing. Life in the middle of the nineteenth century in America was going faster and faster and faster. It was the Age of Progress, the Age of Western Expansion, a time when Americans believed firmly in the "Manifest Destiny" of this new nation. Now railroads, such as the Baltimore & Ohio, and canals linked many cities. The telegraph, clipper ships, even the early sewing machine had been invented by the height of the Album Quilt period. This was also the era of "Cities Beautiful." Monumental architecture was going up in such major cities as Washington, Baltimore, and Philadelphia. There were new religions, new social and benevolent societies, new moral causes such as prohibition, temperance, and abolition. There was war over the annexation of Texas, and the threat of war over the issue of whether territories should be admitted to the Union as slave states or free. So while exciting, these times were also unnerving, unsettling, troubled times. And yet they produced a flowering in American quiltmaking that many now call "classic," setting a standard by which other quiltmaking should be judged.

Might there be some parallels between the mid-nineteenth-century blossoming of Album Quilts and our own of the late twentieth century? I believe so. For the present flowering of quiltmaking, begun in the late 1960s, seems to have stemmed from just this same sort of unsettled times. The present quiltmaking revival may, in part, have been a reaction in America to the troubled era on whose heels it followed. The sixties shook us to the roots with the Cuban missile crisis, man's landing on the moon, the turmoil of desegregation, race riots, Students for a Democratic Society and their terrorist fringes, the birth control pill, the Vietnam War, and the women's rights movement. All these, for better or worse, shook our sense of who we are as a nation. One reaction seems to have been a seeking of comfort and stability in the roots of tradition. The "country look" in home decor came in, and thousands of American women, most of whose mothers had not quilted, harkened back to that craft to produce — in the late twentieth century — quilts of such beauty and in such numbers that this, too, may become a classic period itself.

That Album Quilts once again suit the collecting and conserving mood seems confirmed. But my sense is that we are still learning the style, still savoring its past efflorescence, for this is how classic art is ever learned. Yet we may need to probe the classic construct of these quilts just a bit deeper. For as we strive to understand what they are, and what made them what they are, their beauty and their depth of spirit will inspire us to new visions of our own. And that probing both of form and of philosophical function, after all, is the purpose of these volumes. For one senses that we are only just now beginning to see contemporary Albums taken in directions substantively "beyond Baltimore." A rare few of these quilts, most as yet unfinished, seem close to breaking some aesthetic barrier where the old is reborn into something new, but yet again itself classic. If enough of our Albums reach such heights, we too, will have set a classic standard for the future, a standard for all time.

---

[1] Significant time and talent differences between block construction and quilt completion is shown by later finishing, signaled by the inclusion of sewing machine work, or by quilting which is overly simple, or evenly poorly done, by comparison to the level of most of the appliqué. We also suspect gift of partial sets of blocks or communal help when a number of blocks are signed and presumably sewn by the final recipient of the quilt, as seems the case with the Numsen II Album Quilt discussed later in this series. Certainly some quilts would seem to have been presented to a recipient as completed quilts. One such might be the Baltimore Museum of Art's Album Quilt inscribed "Bible / To / Miss Elizabeth Sliver / This is / Affections tribute Offering — / Presented By Father & Mother / To / Miss Elizabeth Sliver /

Baltimore — 1849." The comparable quality of the appliqué blocks, the set, the quilting and finishing, the very inscription, all bespeak a project begun and completed as a whole, whether by one individual or by many.

[2] William Rush Dunton, Jr., *Old Quilts*, Catonsville, Md., 1946, p. 170.

[3] Barbara Franco, *Fraternally Yours*, Lexington, Mass., Scottish Rite Museum, 1986, p. 10. "By the end of the nineteenth century, in part due to its beneficiary aspects, Odd Fellowship equaled or even outstripped Freemasonry in membership. Many men belonged to both organizations."

PHOTO 2-1. The Rollins Family Record Block, probably New Hampshire, circa 1840. This is a pieced and inked family record bearing the names Ebenezer and Betsy Rollins, among others. Unfinished, it may have been intended as a central medallion to a quilt. 16 ⅞" x 16 ¾". Gift of Mr. & Mrs. Jason Westerfield. (Photo courtesy of the Abby Aldrich Rockefeller Folk Art Center)

Chapter Two
Victorian Inkings

Photo 2-2. *Hearts and Swans II*, appliquéd by Mary Wise Miller, 1989. Pattern #6 in *Baltimore Album Quilts — Historic Notes and Antique Patterns*. Inscribed by Elly Sienkiewicz.

The period from roughly 1840 through the 1870s seems to witness the introduction and the full blossoming of writing and drawing on Album Quilts in India ink. These two arts, Album Quilt making and calligraphy, or "beautiful writing," enhanced each other in the heirloom quilts of the period. So elegant and so successful was this combining of arts that it contributed to the classic heights reached by the Baltimore Album Quilts.

In these quilts, the Victorian inkings often went beyond the written word to include the drawing of fine details on flowers (rose hairs, stamens, the veins on leaves), even to sketches of figures, houses, and public structures. In addition, small, intricate penned insignia (motifs of doves, banners, a fountain, or a house, for example) and an inscription often nestled somewhere on the block. These are particularly delightful to come upon, a bit rare and special, like a freshly spun spider web. As with the Album Quilt block patterns themselves, we don't really know where their tiny signature logos came from. My assumption is that, like ourselves, our needlesisters of yore were always watchful for suitable decorations wherever they might find them. One such banderole ("little banner"), for instance, was found on a Victorian calling card (Figure 2-6). It is virtually the exact match to one on a classic Baltimore Album Quilt. Along with several others, it is included in this chapter.

India ink seems to have been introduced in this country in the 1830s.[1] Within a decade, it overtook embroidery (largely cross-stitch) as the primary method for marking linens. Happily, this coincided with the Victorians' passion for albums of all sorts. There were albums for autographs, signed verses combined with watercolored "remembrances" and other artwork, scriptural quotations, family albums, and "friendship's offerings." It seems quite understandable that quiltmakers with a reliable and easily acquired permanent ink would reflect this same enthusiasm for collections in the Album Quilts of the mid-nineteenth century. As early as the late eighteenth century, according to the Orlofskys in *Quilts in America*, metal dies were manufactured for linen marking in ink. A 1771 New York newspaper ad offered to "cut gentlemen and ladies names, with numbers for numbering linen, and books."[2] To sign their Album Quilts, some Victorian needlewo-

men perfected small hand-drawn signature logos: birds with banderoles, sprays of flowers, and cartouches or decorative borders. Privileged ones had elegantly decorated lead signature stamps or brass and tin signature stencils made. These sewing notions, now treasured antiques, bespeak a time when art needlework was a much admired and popular feminine accomplishment. That there was a market for these signature devices indicates quiltmaking activities of the sort so happily familiar to us today: the custom of block exchanges, and of groups of friends and associates making quilts as gifts to celebrate important occasions.

My sense, though, is that all the elaborate ink sketching and writing that I have seen on Baltimore Album Quilts has been done freehand, perhaps with tracing and the lightest of pencil sketches beneath, but not with stencils or stamps. Commonly, just a name with possibly a date and/or place are written on these quilts. With wonderful frequency, however, there is more. Religious and political expressions, and professions of friendship, are the basic sentiments inscribed. Seemingly most common were phrases such as, "Remember me always" and "When this you see, Remember me." Yet another asks, "Accept my gift affection brings / Though poor the offering be. / It flows from Friendship's purest spring / A tribute let it be."[3] These simple, heartfelt sentiments have lasted into a second century. They assure us that these quilts, these "magic blankets" of hopes, dreams, and memories served their purpose well.

A name, a place, a date excite us in a quilt. They tie us more closely to the maker. They are a clue to the human element in the quilt. If more information is written, we gain insight into our nation's history and into ourselves as well. So much is conveyed in so few words by these nineteenth-century quilt inscriptions: "Presented to Mr. Minor / by the Young Ladies of / Thorndale Seminary,"[4] or, "I'll remember my Angie, whatever betide, I'll think of her always, Tho waters divide."[5] In these we feel the timeless thread of human emotions tying past to present, us to them.

Expressions of fervent patriotism abound in these quilts, but expressions of friendship are more common: "May you be blest with all that Heaven can send, / Long Life, long Health, long Pleasure & a Friend, / May you[r path?] / Angels with their wings display, / And be your guide through every lonely way, / In every clime may you still happy be, / And when far distant / Some times think on me. / Baltimore."[6] We recognize in ourselves this same desire to give our hopes and our beliefs a concrete form, as though the witness of a more tangible medium will help them to come true. Intently, we make of our quilts records of ourselves, our times, the people and things we hold dear. Feeling so strongly then, surely we must include the finishing

Figure 2-1. Roundhand Alphabet by Horace G. Healey. This is one of several engraver's script-style alphabets reminiscent of nineteenth-century quilt inscriptions. The Copperplate pen was pointed but its offset nib gave the thick and thin lines seen here. You can recapture the sensitive line of the vintage Copperplate pen and India ink simply by going back and thickening the downstroke of each letter. (Courtesy of Zaner-Bloser, Inc.)

Rapid Old English

abcdefghijklmnopqrstuvwxyyz

ABCDEFGHIJKLMN

a OPQRSTUVWXYZ s

Profitable. 1234567890 Lettering

Figure 2-2. Rapid Old English from the *The Zanerian Manual of Alphabets and Engrossing.* (Courtesy of Zaner-Bloser, Inc.)

touch of an inscription, even one so simple as a name, a date, a place.

So that your modern heirloom Albums may be as inspired by the possibilities of ink as were those of Old Baltimore, we'll conclude this chapter with some graphic resources. Horace G. Healey's Roundhand Alphabet (Figure 2-1) can be used two ways. Photo 2-2 shows how it looks when I traced each letter directly off this alphabet, first onto paper, then with a lightbox onto fabric using a Pilot™ SCUF pen in brown. Also through the courtesy of the Zaner-Bloser company, a Rapid Old English alphabet (Figure 2-2) is included, as well. See Color Plate 25 in *Volume I* for an example of its usage. Walter J. Filling, a kind friend and noted calligrapher, has graciously made us a series of appropriately Victorian, but nonetheless timeless, words and phrases for tracing onto our quilt blocks. (See Figure 2-3.) Lesson 3 in *Volume I* gives very explicit instructions for how to write on your quilt blocks, how to prepare fabric to stiffen it and to control bleeding, and what pens to use. Re-read it for sure success in your inkwork. The effects of pen and fabric are far too pleasing to be lost to discouragement! Beyond that, there are three techniques to be shared, one for calligraphy, one for signature logos, one for drawing banners.

Technique One:
Recapturing the Copperplate Hand with a Modern Pen

The sort of writing most frequently found in classic Baltimore Album Quilts is a round hand called variously the Copperplate Hand, English Roundhand, or Engraver's Script. The name Spencerian, a similar calligraphy, is also widely used. Roman lettering and counted cross-stitch alphabets are in these quilts as well. Copperplate was done with a pointed pen whose nib was offset from the handle, making it more flexible. Because of this, all of the downstrokes in these alphabets are thicker than the upstrokes. To thicken the line and recapture the Copperplate look, go back over your first tracing of the letters and thicken the downstrokes carefully, one or more times. Even just thickening the downstrokes of your own best schoolgirl penmanship will give it an elegantly calligraphic look. For an example of Copperplate written with modern pens, see Photo 2-3. To see Old English traced, see Photo 2-4. To trace a heavier calligraphy, such as Old English, on your fabric, first draw the letter's outline in a very fine pen, then go back and carefully thicken all its downward strokes.

Technique Two:
Transferring Engraved Signature Logos

While you can trace the basic outline of elegant Victorian cartouches, the fact that they can be photocopied and ironed on may prove very useful. The secret to this is to use freshly made (two hours old

Photo 2-3. *Grapevine Lyre Wreath*, appliquéd, drawn, and inscribed by Elly Sienkiewicz. Inside the wreath, the Pilot™ SCUF pen was used to write with while the Pigma™ SDK pen was used beneath it. The picture is a silhouette of a Hans Christian Andersen landscape framed by a pen-dotted background.

Photo 2-4. *Fleur-de-Lis Medallion II* (Pattern #21 from *Baltimore Album Quilts — Historic Notes and Antique Patterns*). Appliquéd by Georgia Cibul, 1988. Calligraphy by Walter J. Filling, traced onto the block in brown Pilot™ SCUF pen by Elly Sienkiewicz.

or younger) photocopies. Any carbon-based copier should work.

1. Photocopy Figure 2-4.

2. Trim the excess paper off to within an inch of the design.

3. Working on a lightbox, pin the design in place on your fabric. The photocopy should face the right side of the fabric.

4. Now at the ironing board, work on a relatively hard surface (use a cardboard center from a fabric bolt, or a clean, covered bread board). Press hard with a hot (cotton setting) dry iron against the back of the photocopy to transfer it. Practice first. I usually try to accomplish the transfer by just two repositionings of the iron as it's important not to smear the print by moving the paper in the process.

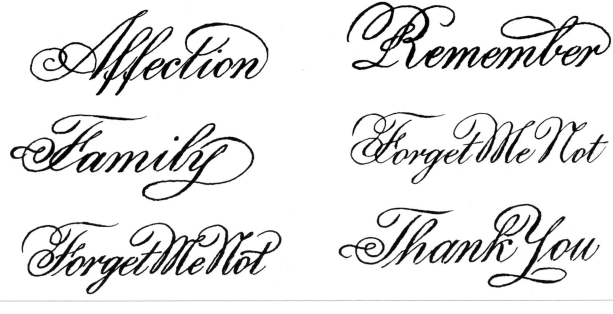

Figure 2-3. Album block inscriptions by Walter J. Filling. Calligraphed especially for this volume at the Filling farm in Emporium, Pennsylvania, July 1989.

5. You should have a clear, though possibly lighter, impression of the engraved design. I am told that this impression will wash off cotton. This doesn't concern me a great deal, though, because the next step is to ink in the design. (I have been advised not to wash antique quilts which have ink on them, and I earnestly hope that the blocks I ink will stay similarly dry.)

6. To ink in the design, I use a Pigma™ set of .01, .03, and .05 black pens. I do the outlines as solid lines, then fill in the "engraving" with tiny dots and short lines. The results are quite fine as you can see in the photos in this chapter. More signature motifs appear in Figure 2-5. Note: Words can also be transferred, but the image on the cloth is the reverse of that on your paper. To come out right, you will have to trace the words upside down on a lightbox. This will give you their mirror image to photocopy.

7. Iron all inkwork to set it.

Photo 2-5. Detail of Jo Anne Parisi's signature logo, 1990; inscribed by Elly Sienkiewicz using both iron-on photocopy transfer and tracing.

Photo 2-6. Detail: Signature emblem on Georganna Clark's block, showing the name written beside the design rather than within a frame or banner. Photocopy transferred design, inked by Elly Sienkiewicz.

Figure 2-4. Samples of simpler cartouches for photocopy transfer. (Courtesy Dover Publications)

Figure 2-5. Additional, more detailed, signature emblems and banderoles. These engraved signature emblems resemble the sort used in the classic quilts. (Courtesy Dover Publications)

Figure 2-6. This same design embellishes both a Victorian calling card and a classic Album Quilt block. (From a private collection)

Technique Three:
Drawing the Banners to Size and Shape

1. First estimate the length of the line needed to accommodate what you wish to write. (See Figure 2-7A.)

2. Fold a sheet of graph paper in half. Then cut the banner on the fold, so that its finished size accommodates the phrase you wish to inscribe on it. (See Figure 2-7B.)

3. Fold the short ends of this paper banner in half lengthwise, and clip out a triangle so that they look like trimmed ribbon ends. (See Figure 2-7C.)

4. Next, simply fold this strip into the banner shape you'd like. (See Figure 2-7D.)

5. Curved banners can also be made this way. (See Figure 2-7E.)

6. For an asymmetrical effect, cut the banner in half on the fold and reassemble the halves with one side flopped over, then tape back on. (See Figure 2-7F.)

7. When the banner pleases you, put it on the lightbox and simply trace this folded three-dimensional banner onto a piece of paper as a one-dimensional drawing. If you choose a softer drawn look, your paper model is still a useful rough outline. Simply make the line more sensitive and flowing than with perfectly straight edges, as you draw it.

Note also that plenty of signatures were simply inscribed next to an embellishing emblem rather than in a frame or banner. (See Photo 2-6.) While paper-cutting for banderoles is full of possibilities, we've been given enough here to take us at least one step further towards the ornate ink embellished elegance of the Victorian Baltimore Album Quilts.

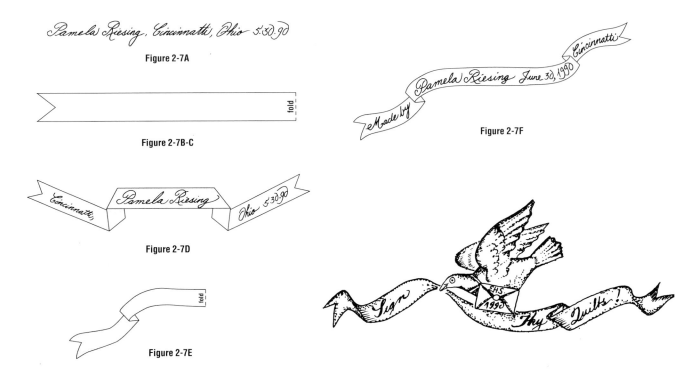

Figure 2-7A

Figure 2-7B-C

Figure 2-7D

Figure 2-7E

Figure 2-7F

---

[1]   William Rush Dunton, Jr., *Notebooks* (unpublished), in the Baltimore Museum of Art. A letter to Dr. Dunton, from Payson's Indelible Ink Co., dated April 18, 1932, reads: "I am very glad to state that so far as we are aware, PAYSON'S is the first indelible ink that came on to the market and met with success almost at once, way back in 1835, so it seems reasonable to suppose that it came into common use somewhere between '35 and '45."

[2]   Peregrine Montague, *The Family Pocketbook: or Fountain of True and Useful Knowledge*, London, (n.d.-18th century), pp. 49-50 (as quoted in Patsy and Myron Orlofsky, *Quilts in America*, New York, McGraw-Hill, 1974, p. 275).

[3]   Inscribed on a Baltimore quilt top made for the Rev. Bernard H. Nadal (1847). Transcribed in the accession notes on quilt #1983.0866.01, courtesy of the Smithsonian Institution, Washington.

[4]   *Old Quilts*, p. 152.

[5]   From an 1846-1847 appliqué Album Quilt inscribed "Baltimore, Maryland" in the collection of Lee Porter. The last line may read, "Tho sisters divide."

[6]   See note 3.

Photo 3-1. *Wyman House*, appliquéd, drawn, and inscribed by Elly Sienkiewicz. Block: Fleur-de-Lis with Rosebuds III (Pattern #13 in *Baltimore Album Quilts — Historic Notes and Antique Patterns*).

Chapter Three
Picture Blocks

Seemingly the rarest blocks, and to me the most fascinating, are those squares which are Album portraits of people, places, and objects. Dr. Dunton called them naturalistic appliqué. "By this," he wrote in the manuscript for his never-published quilt pattern dictionary, "I mean those quilt designs which attempt to reproduce in fabric some semblance of objects seen in daily life, such as, a pump, house, church, etc."[1] We'll call them, more simply, picture blocks.

Are picture blocks unique to the Baltimore-style Album Quilts? Strictly defined, no. On occasion one sees animals, a building, tools, a ship, or a human couple in other nineteenth-century quilts. But in the Baltimore-style Albums, one senses the evolution of a full portrait or "picture" concept — subject matter captured *in situ* and framed by a scene or a decorative border. It is the appearance of this unique picture block concept coincidentally with a well-documented popularity for the early photographic portraits that may, in fact, offer us a better understanding of the Baltimore Album Quilts and the ladies who made them. For by 1845, Baltimore's first daguerreotype studio, one of a chain of fourteen in major American cities, had opened its doors.[2]

The daguerreotype studios specialized in photographic portraits of the local citizenry. For even more then than today, perhaps, permanent separation from one's kith and kin was commonplace. Both a high mortality rate and the tide of migration rent families and friendships asunder. Such separations must have made portraits — human likenesses captured in time and place — especially cherished objects.

In an age that prided itself on technological progress, daguerreotypes, the early French process (introduced to America in 1839 and prevalent until 1850) was readily accepted. It was even greeted with rather effusive enthusiasm, as witnessed by this January 17, 1840, accolade in the *Cincinnati Daily Chronicle*: "That light should be its own historian and draftsman, is, indeed, a sublime conception."[3]

Indeed, these daguerreotypes combined two elements that the Victorian mind considered as sources of truth: the "objectivity of science" and "the pencil of nature." But despite this tie-in to nature and truth, outdoor scenes and buildings are rare among the earliest photographs. In a potentially significant parallel to the Baltimore Album Quilts, the earliest known building portrait in Maryland was of Baltimore's Monument to George Washington, taken in 1842. Album quilts bearing dates such as 1844 or 1845 might well have been begun as early as 1842 or 1843. Then, too, Baltimore's War of 1812 Battle Monument was the second Maryland building photographed. Along with the first photographic portrait of the United States Capitol, the latter picture was made in 1846. Notably rare as well are the "picture blocks," squares portraying people, places, and everyday things, in the Baltimore Album Quilts. And among the building images thus decorating these quilts, the Baltimore Monument to George Washington seems the most often portrayed, followed by the War of 1812 Memorial, and then the U.S. Capitol.

Perhaps it is just coincidence that these two types of buildings, photographic and stitchery, flourished side by side in Baltimore in the middle of the nineteenth century. But it is intriguing to note a further common element: the same sort of filigree cutouts that frame some daguerreotypes in metal, frame at least one Album Quilt block in appliquéd fabric. Matthew Brady was one of the first to manufacture those ornate shadow-box frames, cases that both protected and elegantly presented daguerreotypes. Then working for a jewelry store, the entrepreneurial Brady began frame production in 1843. One is struck by the similarity — both in concept and appearance — between the red appliquéd frame on the antique block "Hunting Scene" (block E-1, quilt #10) and those jewelry-like daguerreotype cases.

Without words, picture blocks tell us much about civic pride, patriotism, Baltimore's role in the nation's history, enthusiasm for the new technology of the Age of Progress, and also suggest visions of tranquility, both pastoral and domestic. The concept of picture blocks is among the most expressive of our Baltimore Album Quilt heritage. Given this, what might you so portray in your quilt? For my part, some of my earliest Album blocks were picture blocks depicting our house and family. Two blocks, shown in Color Plates 4 and 5, feature my daughter Katya and her parents. Her brothers, Donald and Alex, are represented in the same quilt,

Photo 3-2. Detail: *Wyman House*, drawn and inscribed by Elly Sienkiewicz. This picture block is an example of a traced drawing of a building. The picture's outline appears to have then been "engraved" or "etched" by various repeated pen strokes.

shown in *Volume I's* quilt #6, by two classic replicas based on the hunting scene mentioned earlier. Exerting the magic power which every quilter has, I bordered the square portrait of myself and my husband (Color Plate 4) with a frame of acorns and oak leaves. For in the language of flowers, acorns symbolize Longevity, and oak leaves symbolize Courage. Ernest Hemingway characterized courage as "grace under pressure," something we all have need of now and then.

To consider designing our own picture blocks, we need to analyze them a bit further, the better to understand how the classic examples were conceived. To begin, one could categorize the Album picture blocks into two types:

I. *Wreathed portraits.* Here, the portrayed subject is depicted silhouetted against the block's background cloth and framed by some floral border or wreath. The "border" may be as little as the floral garland under the clipper ship, shown in Block C-3 in Photo 4-11. Or the border may consist of more of a frame, such as the wreath in Photo 3-3. The back cover's "Queen of May" block is an excellent classic example of a wreath-framed portrait, as are blocks B-5 and D-3 in quilt #6 in the Color Section.

II. *Scenery blocks.* Here the picture block is a full scene, like a photograph or painting. These vintage portraits appear two ways:

A. Framed in cutwork appliqué. The picture is presented in a *scherenschnitte*-designed frame. This is very rare; block E-1 in quilt #10 in the Color Section is the only classic example that comes to mind. Jean Wells Keenan's block (Photo 3-4) and Sally Glaze's in Color Plate 3 are similarly framed by *scherenschnitte* borders.

B. Self-framed. The picture is presented framed, but the frame consists of elements within the picture itself, as seen in Photo 3-5. Here the open sky is bordered in by leaves and birds, while lawn and trees frame the three other sides of the picture.

Now, let's look at these two types of picture blocks more closely. The first, the wreathed portrait, is simple enough. It uses the basic vocabulary of Album block design. As you observe this picture-block style in the Gallery Quilts, you will find it relatively easy to conceive of putting a picture of your choosing into your own Album Quilt, just as I did in the cover blocks for *Volume I.* Your choices are to appliqué the picture into the frame, or to ink it into the frame. Or both. The figures in quilt #6 in the Color Section, in blocks B-5 and D-3, appear to be of the rare sort that have appliquéd clothes, but inked and watercolored features. Another seemingly unique portrait is labeled "Queen of May," a graceful ink-drawn and paint-washed figure within a lyre wreath, block C-2 in quilt #10 in the Color Section. Similarly, inked pictures of a house or of a spring occur, but rarely, in the Baltimore Album Quilts.

The Odense Album, quilt #17 in the Color Section, has quite a display of inked "beyond Baltimore" picture blocks. Patterns for it appear in *Baltimore Album Quilts — Historic Notes and Antique Patterns.* In all cases, the frames of these are simpler than the layered wreaths found round inked pictures in classic Baltimore Albums. Let's go through the steps for how a similar contemporary inked picture block, "Wyman House" (Photo 3-1) would have been constructed:

1. Appliqué a block with a center suitably open for an inked picture. Wyman House is drawn into the pattern Fleur-de-Lis with Rosebuds III. (See Pattern #13 in *Baltimore Album Quilts — Historic Notes and Antique Patterns.*) In this volume, Patterns #6 and #7 would be suitable for framing an inked or appliquéd picture.

2. Iron your block, right side down on a fluffy towel, using Magic Sizing™ spray starch on the wrong side. This stiffens the fabric so it's easier to draw on and inhibits the ink from bleeding.

3. Prepare a pencil line drawing of your picture on graph paper. To do this, photo-reduce a drawn

or photographed picture to size, then trace a drawing of the major architectural and landscape features onto graph paper. Next, take one of the permanent pens you will be using on the block itself and go over your pencil lines in ink on the graph paper. This does two things: one, it gives you practice in drawing with that pen. Two, photographs must be thus simplified and the lines darkened, so that their shapes are clear enough to trace through fabric. This is also your chance to gauge how effective your final drawing on fabric will be. Any writing captioning the picture on the block should now also be done on this paper, first in pencil, then in ink. Note: Wyman House was drawn using a black Pigma™ pen set in sizes .01, .03, and .05. The outlines of the drawing were done first, using a six-inch gridded C-Thru™ ruler to keep the building lines straight and true.

4. Working on a lightbox, pin the drawing, right side up, to the back of the appliquéd block which is also right side up. Keep a second copy of the drawing out and visible. It will be useful to see the picture without the fabric.

5. Once you have a good outline drawing inked on the block, you are ready to "engrave" it. Engraving is how I think of all the little lines and dots which are my tools for shading and filling in of the drawing — and which, in fact, look like engraving. (For this look, see Photo 3-2.) While a photo or a charcoal sketch has gray tones, you, like an engraver, have only black ink or white background to establish your scene. Your engraving strokes are these fillers: short horizontal, vertical, diagonal, or cross-hatched lines (good for brickwork and slate roofs), squiggly, scribbly lines (good for stonework and shrubbery), and shading lines or filler lines taken very lightly and rapidly, right next to each other in an area. It will feel as though you are chicken-scratching the cloth. One layer of strokes should gray-in an area, the next layer should darken it more. Layered, radiating zigzag lines make good foliage. And last, but my favorite, are dots — hundreds of filler dots graduating from very condensed to more widely spaced. Dots are easy to control, and effective — but tedious.

6. Turn the lightbox off periodically to check your progress. And that's all there is to it. If you're very unsure, practice. You could, of course, always ink first, appliqué second. I guess I've always enjoyed seeing the picture go centered, right into its frame. Which is not to say that I haven't investigated how the block's center could be replaced in case of failure!

Photo 3-3. *Gone with the Wind*, designed and appliquéd by Rena Hefley, 1988. No pattern. This is a charmingly simple example of a picture block whose figures are framed by a wreath.

Let's now consider the second type of picture blocks, the scenery blocks. We'll approach the matter with questions and answers. We'll investigate first the *scherenschnitte*-framed blocks and second, the self-framed blocks.

A. What characterizes a successful **scherenschnitte-bordered block?** The ideal scherenschnitte ("scissors-cutting") border design integrates a scenery block into the mixed-style blocks of a classic Album Quilt. The outside edge of the scherenschnitte border (quilt #10, block E-1) is scalloped with graceful compass-point corners. It incorporates the background cloth, tying this block both to its border and to other blocks in the quilt. This frame has a characteristic Baltimore-style airiness to it. Its center is a square on point, medallion style. The diagonal lines give the impression of motion, as diagonal lines do best, and they focus the eye on the central scene inside. Small gold candy-drop motifs add a bright second color, leading gracefully into the multicolored scene inside.

B. How can I design my own **scherenschnitte border frame?** The following paper-fold method leaves a medallion center open for a scene, a figure, or even an inscription. If symbolism appeals to you, list symbols which convey an appropriate meaning for your block. It will start the creative process and may be the source of a great design! Thus, hearts, meaning Love or Devotion, provided an appropriate symbol to border round our daughter Katya in Color

Photo 3-4. *Duty, Honor, Country*, designed and appliquéd by Jean Wells Keenan, 1989-1990. His mother looked forward to having Pvt. Jason Frederick Wells home for Christmas 1989. Instead he was deployed to Panama City on Christmas Eve day to help roust Noriega. Missing him, she worked an Album block by which to remember the event. The patriotic young soldier is depicted here, flag in hand, framed by the classic *scherenschnitte* picture-block border. He returned from Panama safely, January 26, 1990.

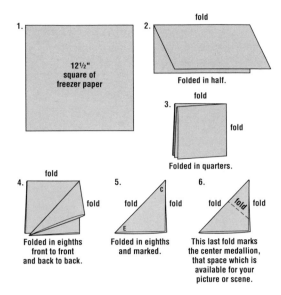

Figure 3-1. Paper-folding for a medallion-centered cutwork appliqué frame.

Plate 5. You may also want to make a list of subjects to portray in your own picture blocks. Such a preliminary listing can sometimes precipitate the appearance of a serendipitous picture-block concept.

Paper-folding for a medallion-centered frame:

1. Cut a 12½" square of freezer paper. This is your finished block size.
2. Fold this square in half, shiny side inside, top to bottom. (See Figure 3-1.)
3. Fold the square into fourths, folding right to left.
4. Then fold the square into eighths, folding the front to the front, and the back to the back.
5. Mark this eighth which faces you. Mark "C" at the center where all the folds meet. Mark "E" in the lower left-hand corner to indicate edges.
6. To ensure a medallion "window," make one more fold, folding the upper corner (C) one third of the way down the hypotenuse. The distance from the upper point to this last fold determines the size of the window. The closer to the upper point, the smaller the window; the further away, the larger the window. Open the square up to see what you've created.

7. Refold the paper in preparation to draw on your design.

C. How do I place my design motif to make a frame?
The successful *scherenschnitte* frames pictured in this volume have these characteristics:

1. An outer edge with cutouts to soften the frame's connection to the background fabric.
2. Interior cuts to integrate the frame and give it interest and airiness.
3. A pretty medallion window shape.
4. The dominant design interest is along the hypotenuse, but a significant secondary design centers on the shorter fold as well.
5. The design must be attached from the left folded edge to the right folded edge. This is the same principle we all followed in our childhood: the paper dolls had to hold hands from one fold to the other fold of our accordioned paper. If we can recapture a bit of the relaxed attitude of that time, the designing of *scherenschnitte* frames can become as pleasurable as child's play!

I've included a couple of such frame shape suggestions, just for inspiration. (See Figures 3-2A-C.) To view them completed, you'll have to fold, draw, staple, and cut, following the preceding instructions. And, then, I believe, there'll be no stopping dozens of your own designs from crowding into your imagination and flowing out your fingertips.

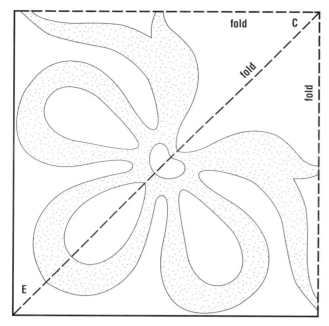

Figure 3-2A

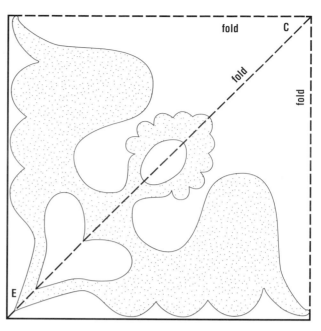

Figure 3-2B

Figure 3-2A-C. These are pattern sketches of medallion-centered blocks designed by the author. After following this chapter's instructions for recreating a heart medallion frame, similar to Pattern #7, try to paper-fold and cut some of these designs. If this appeals, you will love *Volume III* whose focus is on paper-cut appliqué quilts.

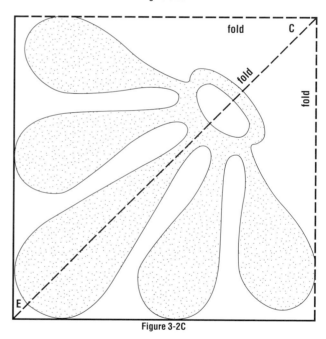

Figure 3-2C

D. How could I make a heart medallion frame freehand? To better understand how these frames evolve, draw freehand a heart medallion frame (a variation of Pattern #7) on the paper square you have just folded:

1. Draw one large half-heart on the hypotenuse, as shown in Figure 3-3A.

2. Draw a second, smaller heart on the vertical fold, as shown in Figure 3-3B. That this heart impinges on the center picture medallion gives it an interesting and pretty frame shape. It makes the interior square opening set square rather than on point.

3. Draw an interior cutout on each heart. (See Figure 3-3C.)

4. Doublecheck that the two hearts touch and are attached. This keeps the folds attached. Staple inside the heart in a couple of places to keep the layers from shifting. Cut along the top edge of the design from fold to fold. Next cut the bottom edge of the design from fold to fold. Last cut the interior designs. Cut one shape out of the right side, then one shape out of the left side.

5. Unfold the pattern and take a critical look. Can anything be redrawn and cut to make it more

visually pleasing? And then the important question: What, if anything, needs to be modified to make this block frame easier to appliqué? With these considerations in mind, fold, draw, and cut a final pattern.

Additional motifs such as the yellow candy-drop motif on Pattern #7 can be added for interest. Proceed with the freezer-paper-on-top method of cutwork appliqué from *Volume I*, Lesson 2. In addition to those instructions, please note: The iron must be dry and almost scorching hot, and great pressure must be used on points to make the pattern adhere sufficiently well to the right side of the fabric.

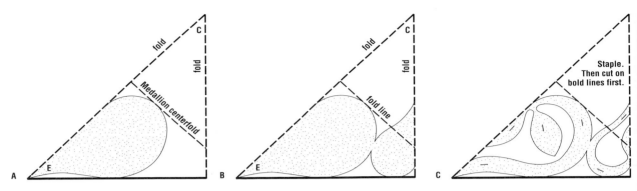

Figure 3-3A-C. Freehand drawing of the Heart Medallion Frame. Recreating this frame, so similar to Pattern #7, will reinforce the method for making your own original design blocks in this picture medallion style. (A) Draw a large heart on the hypotenuse. (B) Draw a smaller heart adjacent to the first heart. Draw this smaller heart upside down, cen- tered on the short fold. Erase the line between the two hearts to remind you not to cut them apart. (C) After drawing an interior design such as leaves, staple, then cut. Cut the outside lines of the design first, then the inner lines.

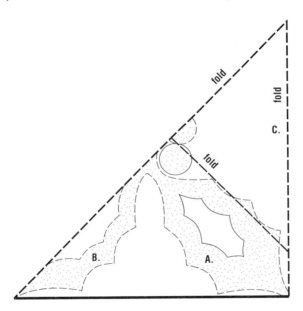

Figure 3-4A-C. Creating a sample botanical medallion frame: a holly border. A. The same holly leaf is repeated to form the pattern. B. The leaf with berries is the focus of the design and is placed on the long fold. C. A second leaf touches the short fold to hold the pattern together and to create a medallion frame.

(Should it then stick so well that it is difficult to remove, rewarm the paper with the iron. Lift the paper with tweezers, being careful not to shred the top layer of paper off separately.)

E. What principles do I need to know to make a botanical block frame like the Acorn and Oak Leaf Frame? Botanical motifs are a step more challenging than the hearts. But because they can be made by following a formula, they may open up a multitude of original designs for you. In designing Pattern #6, Acorn and Oak Leaf Frame, I decided that I needed a symmetrical oak leaf template, so I made one by cutting a leaf on a fold. With a bit of adjusting, I got one

which fit so that the long fold on the left was attached to the short fold on the right. Because in my designs the focus of interest seems always to be in the corners, I placed the acorn motif itself on the long fold. One of the important lessons in this particular study is that one unit of the design can be created separately (as the oak leaf was), then incorporated as you draw the design onto the folded pattern paper. This gives you more versatility. Play with this botanical concept a bit. Imagine other plants which would be pretty, from something as simple as a tulip, to something as seasonal as holly. Then follow these steps:

1. Choose your plant. Simplify its representation, cutting repeated units, like a leaf, separately as tracing templates.

2. Draw the focus of the design on the long fold, where there is more space.

3. Make some element of the design — a leaf, a petal, even a butterfly — touch the short fold of the pattern paper. Make sure the design attaches the short fold to the long fold. This holds the frame together. (See Figure 3-4A-C.)

F. How can I simplify a scene so I can show it in appliqué? Have in your mind's eye what you want to show. Decide whether you want a densely appliquéd block with little background showing, or a lighter block incorporating more background. At this point, you can consider how to deal with elements such as perspective in simplifying your picture block scene for appliqué.

Perspective made very simple: Imagine a glass window, a "picture plane," through which the scene is viewed. Divide the scene into three picture planes: the foreground, the middle-ground, and the background. The horizon or vanishing point might be shown, as in "Tropical Boating" (Color Plate 12)

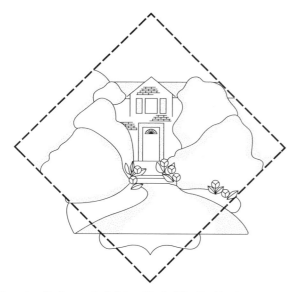

Figure 3-5. Background of picture block, "The Sienkiewiczes at Home," illustrating simple perspective built by minimal picture planes.

Figure 3-6. Foreground of picture block, "The Sienkiewiczes at Home," illustrating simple figure portrayal. The foreground is always shown on a larger scale than the background to help create the illusion of perspective.

where it lies beyond the boat, as far as the eye can see. But in most Album block scenes it can't be seen because something blocks the view, as in "Goose Girl" (Photo 3-5).

Sometimes there are only two picture planes, background and foreground (Figures 3-5 and 3-6). In "The Sienkiewiczes at Home" (Color Plate 4), the couple is shown large in the front, and the house is in the back. Perspective is created by two things. First, size: big couple in front, small house behind; and second, a receding line, the path, that gets smaller as it traverses the foreground to the background and is stopped by the house.

Simplifying the scene's elements: Everything in "The Sienkiewiczes at Home" has been simplified. The house is portrayed as you would describe its major visible characteristics: brick, peaked dormer over second-floor window, red door (Figure 3-5). There are trees flanking the front center and they have arbitrarily been brought together thickly to eliminate the need to show more detail. In cases where a building takes up most of the block, a bit of flora ornamentation may adorn it, as with a garden. Often the same stylistic distortion of proportion that we see in earlier samplers occurs here: flowers tower over houses, "giant" birds perch on roofs. With an old needleart conceit, in this block as in the "Goose Girl" block, flowers are shown oversize as a decorative element.

Figure 3-7. Acorn and Oak Leaf Frame, Pattern #6. Cutwork appliqué picture-block frames may be made first, leaving the inner seams unsewn to accommodate insertion of the scene (see Lesson 1 in *Volume I*). Alternatively, they may be put on after the scene is sewn in place if one irons the frame's freezer paper pattern onto the frame fabric, then trims back to the seam allowance. This gives you the necessary visibility to center the frame over the appliquéd picture. Then baste the frame carefully in place before appliquéing with the freezer paper pattern left on top. (See Lesson 2 in *Volume I*.)

People

Human figures are exceptions in the classic Baltimore Album Quilts. Birds and butterflies, for exam-ple, are much more common. If you want to include people, but feel you can't possibly draw the human figure, look for simplified pictures as a resource. Check folk-art books or needleart books. Even children's coloring books may help. People are difficult for me, too. I try to draw them out as what I call "egg people," constructed of ovals. Art stores carry jointed wooden figures based on this principle and you can pose them as you like.

I usually do many, many sketches for a figured picture block. I trace off the best parts of the drawing and try again. From sketching the basic shapes in ovals, I proceed to clothing, then to features. In costume, I try to dress family members in clothes we actually own but that look a bit timeless, or even old-fashioned. So I put my daughter in the then-fashionable midi-length jumper and leg warmers. My husband is in the time-honored business suit, and I am in a very serviceable old gold dress which has stood by me for over a decade of last-minute official functions. On the block, both the dress and I look younger and brighter than we now appear, but as quiltmakers, that is both our privilege and our power — to depict ourselves not necessarily as we are, but as we would like to be remembered.

Photo 3-5. *Goose Girl*, appliquéd by Donna Collins, 1989. Though picture blocks are rare, this pastoral scene is repeated several times. In one version, the house, fenced garden, tree, and goose-inhabited pond are there but instead of the bonneted lady, a folded silk beehive is a- swarm with busy bees. A separately framed block, family lore says it was "kept from the quilt because the maker was an artist." The repetition of this picture block's theme arouses curiosity about its origins and intent.

Buildings

To make a building, it is easiest to draw it full face forward on graph paper. Simplify it as though for a coloring book, but include selected specifics: shadowed gables, window panes, steps, shutters, the intimation of bricks, or smoke from a chimney. Some superb classic building portraits can be seen in *Volume I's* quilt #2 and in *Baltimore Album Quilts — Historic Notes and Antique Patterns.*

Fabric

With the detailed closeup pictures in these volumes, perhaps little more needs to be said about fabric. But do study the fabric use, particularly the shaded rainbow fabric that adds both the realism of perspective and the delicacy of translucent watercolors to these blocks. Look at "Waterfowling" on the back cover and note how the old rainbow fabric — in varying saturations of color — gives contour to figures, depth to the foliage, perspective to the water. Modern hand-dyed fabrics seem best to imitate this watercolor effect; and several sources providing

these are listed in the Appendix. When scrutinizing the vintage cover blocks, note how economically prints are used to convey layered flowers, and how the inking enhances pictorial detail. Just as multiple classic blocks combine inked detail with appliquéd depictions, you could pen a building or other scenery as background with figures appliquéd on in the foreground. In a sense, it is particularly exciting for us that while the classic Albums give us the concept of picture blocks, they only begin to suggest the possibilities which that particular pattern genre holds for us.

I find it especially helpful to cut my sketched scenery block shapes out of paper and to build up a cut-paper layout of my block design. For me, this comes more easily than drawing a scene in one fell swoop. It also helps me better understand the construction of the scene in fabric which will follow. Note which elements are more easily appliquéd into a larger unit before being sewn down to the background fabric. After a cut-paper scene is laid out, trace it, using a lightbox, onto a sheet of paper. These blocks don't come easily. But no other blocks are quite so worthwhile, or give quite such vivid clues to the life and times of the maker. And no other blocks stir quite as much excitement in the eyes of the viewer as do picture blocks, then as now.

---

1 Dunton, *Notebooks,* in "N" section of letter files.

2 Reese V. Jenkins, *Images and Enterprise: Technology and the American Photographic Industry, 1839-1925,* Baltimore, Johns Hopkins University Press, 1975, p. 18.

3 As quoted in Mame and Marion E. Warren, *Maryland Time Exposures, 1840-1940,* Baltimore, Johns Hopkins University Press, 1984, p. xxi.

Photo 4-1. Baltimore Album Top, signed variously and inscribed *Baltimore* and with various March dates in 1844. Glazed chintz appliqués, blue "resist dyed tabby weave borders." 74¹¹⁄₁₆" x 74⅜". Gift of Mrs. Eugenie Papin Thomas, St. Louis, Missouri. St. Louis Art Museum.

This Album, all of chintz appliqués, seems to mark a transition between the chintz medallion quilts and the Baltimore-style appliquéd Albums featuring a block grid and layered appliqués.

The Quilt Gallery

Welcome to the Quilt Gallery of *Baltimore Beauties and Beyond, Volume II*. This Gallery of black-and-white photos is augmented by those in the Color Section. The fifty-three quilts pictured in this volume offer us a small shared basis upon which to make some observations. While the full extent of the Baltimore Album Quilt genre is not really known, we can speculate a bit about how this style developed and what some of its characteristics seem to be. In Chapter 5, we'll begin a list of observed characteristics with an eye to designing our own quilts and conclude there with a simple "Edging Border" technique. After reading Chapter 5, you'll undoubtedly want to walk back through this and other Galleries, adding your own observations to mine. Fascinated as we are, this process of shared observations is important, for therein lies our best hope of understanding these quilts better. Such study gives pleasure and together we may help answer the questions, Who made these quilts? and Why mid-nineteenth-century Baltimore?

As the eighteenth turned to the nineteenth century, Baltimore was already a prosperous seaport. This was in contrast to nearby Washington. The capital was still considered a hardship post to foreign ambassadors; its mud, mosquitoes, and crowded boarding houses were all too much a part of public servant life there. By the mid-nineteenth century, though, urban, urbane Baltimore already had a long and impressive fancy-work appliqué quilt tradition. What we know of these earlier Maryland fancy quilts seems to imply a smooth transition from an enlarged center medallion style into the Album style based, for the most part, on a regular block unit grid. Let's look briefly at what came before the "Baltimore Album" style, then, and see if we can find a hint as to its origins.

In *Old Quilts*, his study of predominantly Maryland quilts, Dr. William Dunton has a chapter on chintz quilts, those made of "printed glazed calico, or chintz as it is better known."[1] He shows a number of these quilts believed to have originated in the Baltimore/Maryland area and dating from the early decades of the nineteenth century (the dates 1810 and 1825 being specifically mentioned). These would have been among the fancywork quilts which preceded the Baltimore Album Quilts and their aesthetic influence on the latter seems apparent. The solid

printed chintz borders often found on the chintz medallion quilts can be found on classic Baltimore Album Quilts, as can the style of fine overall repeat pattern quilting. Dunton describes one such pattern as "paired lines crossing each other diagonally."

Dunton notes also the pattern of diamonds which was the effect of Marseilles cloth, a heavier fabric which he records as the background on which the cutout chintz was arranged in an overall pattern. When appliquéd to such a background, the complex printed shapes stand out in dramatic contrast to the repetitious geometric background. Subsequently, this look of complex appliqué above an overall quilting pattern (which generally stopped at the appliqué's edge) became a favorite conceit in the classic Baltimore Album Quilts. Though rarely, some representational motifs are created by reverse appliqué in combination with the chintzwork, as shown in Photo 4-3. Reverse appliqué is rare in the Albums, too, occurring, in my experience, on feather-wreathed blocks or borders. And where piecing is present amid the appliqués in these chintz quilts, one sees it most prominently on the symbolically significant star motif. So, too, with piecing in the Albums.

Similarly, the whole aesthetic of the medallion-centered quilt seems to have affected the evolution of the most sophisticated Baltimore Album Quilt style. The style of the elegant chintz medallions is open, airy, and graceful. Small, carefully cut chintz motifs were arranged to form large overall quilt patterns of foliage-linked festoons round central bouquets. In another traditional set, garlanded circular centers are surrounded by squared-off bordering garlands. So too, some elegant later Baltimore Album Quilts show a successful effort to organize the blocks into medallion centers. Notably, some of these center blocks are also festooned by swag-shaped garlands. Such a style may be exuberantly reflected by the quilts in Photos 4-24, 4-25, 4-26, and 4-27. Certainly the informed and inspired print use, the airy open-style sets, and the realistically depicted subject matter (printed on the chintzes, but recreated in layered appliqué in the Albums) can be traced back to these earlier chintz quilts so popular in the Baltimore area before the Album Quilts.

Beyond any interest in ascribing the influence of a particular artist or artists to the Baltimore Album

Quilts, I am struck by how much in these quilts seems to be part of a developing artistic concept in quiltmaking. Consider a rough chronological layout of Baltimore-style Album Quilts such as that in the museum catalog, *Baltimore Album Quilts*. Turning its pages, one is struck by how this appliquéd Album Quilt style seemed to evolve from spontaneously random collections of appliquéd blocks (some in the chintz-work style, some one-layered *scherenschnitte* style, some traditional crossed sprays and wreaths, some in an evolving, quite realistic, Victorian style, some creatively representational of cultural artifacts) into an often much more carefully planned overall style. Approaches which begin to impose a more ordered overall pattern on the set of these Album Quilt blocks include the following:

1. Often the center block becomes a focal point. One wonders if the person whose name it carries or its other inscriptions might be particularly significant. Frequently the center nine blocks in a 25-block set contain the most ornate blocks in a quilt. These are the ones which would show most when the quilt covered a bed.

2. In many quilts, the diagonal lines which bisect the quilt from corner to corner become emphasized. Sometimes this begins by carefully choosing strong diagonal designs such as crossed pine cones or the diagonally placed cornucopia for the four outermost corner blocks.

3. Wreath blocks attract attention in an overall set because of the amount of their open white space. One senses an increased reliance on the open wreaths to set up a strong diagonal movement and to create a center square-on-point medallion focusing on the center block framed within it. We'll point out this style on our Gallery tour.

4. Another medallion center effect is found in those quilts made entirely of the quite realistic, ornately Victorian-style blocks. The inner border features four double-size blocks, while the outer border consists of regular-size blocks. You'll see this in the reproduction quilt, quilt #14 in the Color Section. The quilt squares themselves form the double borders around the center block. Clearly the set of such a quilt has been very carefully thought out and seemingly occurs towards the apex of the Baltimore Album Quilt style.

5. As in the chintz quilt tradition, interior borders are important, whether made up of running (attached motif) appliqués as in Photo 4-27 or made up of blocks.

6. Interior motifs (squares, Greek crosses, crossed diagonals, squares on point) were often created by the arrangement of the blocks themselves. We'll seek these out in the Gallery. In addition, factors such as density of appliqué or color (see quilt #2 in the Color Section) create interior pattern in some of these quilts.

7. Sashing strips were a time-honored means of tying the blocks of a quilt together. One sometimes sees this in the chintz quilts and in some classic Baltimore Album Quilts as well. So, too, outer borders give unity to a quilt and this mode was used effectively both in the earlier chintz quilts and in the classic Baltimore Album Quilts.

Now, all these things being noted, let's move right on into the Quilt Gallery together.

Note: Throughout the photo citations in this section, quoted material is from the descriptive information in the printed acquisition notes or quilt descriptions of the museum, auction house, or owner. Locations of museums are noted only the first time they are cited. Photos are courtesy of the owning agency, unless otherwise noted.

Photo 4-2. "Chintz Quilt, Mrs. William Dimond, Baltimore, Maryland, circa 1820." Approximately 112″ x 114″. (Photo © 1989, Sotheby's, Inc.)

Great numbers of appliquéd chintz medallion quilts from the Baltimore area survive from the early decades of the nineteenth century. Just one is included here to acquaint us with the fancy quilt tradition from which the Baltimore Album Quilts emerged. (Dr. Dunton's *Old Quilts* has many more.) What characteristics of these earlier quilts seem to have influenced the mid-nineteenth-century Albums? One recognizes the central medallion concept, the use of elegant imported prints, the combining of geometric shapes (triangles, diamonds, stars) with representational eighteenth-century border elements such as the bow and scalloped hammock (or swag), the use of chintz cutouts, and the airy, open aspect of the set.

Photo 4-3. Appliquéd Medallion Quilt, "Anna Catherine Hummell Markey, Frederick County, Maryland, circa 1825." 92" x 90⅛". The Daughters of the American Revolution Museum, Washington, D.C.; gift of Mrs. Stephen J. Buynitsky.

This relatively early Maryland quilt evinces quiltmaking traditions which hold even in the ensuing Baltimore-style Album years: the wide-based triangle or "dogtooth" border; the combining of appliqué with reverse appliqué; printed chintz shapes, cutout, with representational shapes made from scratch; and the emphasis on symbolism in subject matter. It's a fine example of a medallion style, but at this point it's not yet based on the grid of squares which comes to characterize even medallion-centered Albums. One senses, though, a strong pull within the Baltimore/Maryland Albums as a whole, to organize the internal pattern of the block design in some graphic way.

Photo 4-4. Appliquéd Medallion Chintz-work Quilt, "New England, 1820-1840." Approximately 102" x 102". (Photo © 1989, Sotheby's, Inc.)

Ostensibly quite far "beyond" Maryland, this early quilt nonetheless reflects many of the same needlework traditions as do Maryland quilts of this vintage. It is its charming edging border, though, that guaranteed it a place in our Quilt Gallery. Draperylike, simple to appliqué, and effective, this Canopy of Heaven Border, as I've dubbed it, appears as Pattern #33 in the pattern section. The Masons used a "cloud canopy" to depict the omnipresence of Heaven, and drapery from above seems a recognizable element in fraktur and German-American folk portraiture of the period. Beyond that, I believe our Baltimorean needlesisters would have liked this border!

Photo 4-5. Album Quilt, from the collection of the Maryland Historical Society. 43½" x 42". Accession #44.88.1.

Perhaps a baby quilt, this vintage piece suggests a short route to a "beyond Baltimore" beauty! It is interesting to note that the two repeated blocks here occur frequently in other Maryland quilts. These possibly fleur-de-lis and maple-leaf motifs resemble those in the quilt on page 8, for example.

Photo 4-6. "Oxford Female Seminary Album Quilt, 1846." 100" x 100". Chester County Historical Society, West Chester, Pennsylvania; gift of Mrs. Conrad Ralston. Accession #1985.17.

This, appropriately, has much more of a Delaware-New Jersey-Pennsylvania look than Baltimore. But blocks in this quilt appear in Baltimore quilts as well. Both of the distinctive grapevine blocks, for example, occur, though infrequently, in Baltimore Album Quilts. The relationship of female seminaries to the migration of designs in the Album Quilts is an intriguing one to speculate upon. As noted in *Quilted for Friends* (p. 34), "The Oxford Female Society was founded in 1837 for the purpose of training young women for the teaching profession. An 1841 school brochure listed required courses, among them reading, plain and ornamental penmanship, English grammar, composition, general history, algebra, botany, Biblical, Grecian, and Roman antiquities, intellectual and moral philosophy, rhetoric, and logic. This quilt was made as a farewell present for the seminary's departing principal and teacher, the Reverend James Grier Ralston."

Photo 4-7. Baltimore Album Quilt, inscribed in part, *Balt*, *1845*, *1846*, and *1847*. 96¼" x 99⅜". (Photo courtesy of the United Methodist Historical Society, Lovely Lane Museum, Baltimore, Maryland)

Looking very much like a group-made quilt, this one offers great opportunities for learning. There are some real gems among its blocks, but their organization lacks dynamism and impact. Blocks C-3 and F-2 are terrific examples of picture blocks. In the latter, we see scene-setting details (the birds and anchor, and possibly a buoy) exaggerated in size. In block C-3, the water's edge is graphically quilted in waves. Another ingenious touch is on the church itself: a small architectural detail print (like a strip of marching brown commas) is used with great realism. It is used similarly in quilt #2 in *Baltimore Album Quilts — Historic Notes and Antique Patterns*. Block C-4 raises interesting questions. Its anchors are virtually exact replicas of that shown in *The True Masonic Chart* under the Mark Mason degree.[2] Note: This is quilt #7 in *Baltimore Album Quilts* by Dena Katzenberg. Its description there lists all the quilt's inscriptions and includes research into the Bethel Seamen's Mission (block C-3), the ship *Hope*, and Reverend and Mrs. Hezekiel Best who presided at that church until 1847.[3]

Photo 4-8. Album Quilt, "Carmelia Everhart (b. 1835), Manchester, Carroll County, Maryland, circa 1857-1859." 81" x 79". The Daughters of the American Revolution Museum; gift of Dr. Kate I. Leatherman.

Though in much the same set, block to block, as the previous quilt, this one seems more successful as an appealing whole. None of its blocks individually are as elegant as the finest in Photo 4-7, but their display makes it, to me, a more visually appealing quilt. The blocks are balanced and quite uniform in the space taken up by the appliqués. They have the aspect of having been designed by one maker. A narrow, but almost regular, white space runs between the blocks and a plain white border and binding makes a surprisingly effective frame to this 16-block set. Without the border, this would clearly be less of a quilt. The quilting contains an elegant serpentine feather border and is worth studying with a magnifying glass.

Photo 4-9. Baltimore Album Quilt (quilt #8 in the Color Section) included here in a watercolor rendering to show the separate sashings cut of background fabric and the quilting pattern. Index of American Design, National Gallery of Art, Washington, D.C. #1943.8.; NYS-te-43.

Note the simple three-stripped border. It looks as though there has been an attempt to organize the round wreaths into a square-on-point medallion shape around a Greek cross formed by baskets. See, though, how much more clearly one can read this internal pattern in another bird-centered quilt, quilt #9 in the Color Section. Particularly intriguing to me is the fact that what are unquestionably quilted acorns are falling from the red-fruited tree in block D-1. This being the case, it may be that acorns are being represented in the hearts of spiky leaves and red circles such as block E-4 in Photo 4-10. Shown so often near what appear to be memorial blocks, this pattern may represent the live oak and fallen heroes in the war over Texas. Here, however, the more common symbolism for the oak seems more likely intended. *Spoken Without a Word* cites these meanings for the oak tree: Hospitality, Stability, Strength of Faith and Virtue, and Symbol of a Christian's Strength against Adversity.[4]

Photo 4-10. Album Quilt, "Beary Family, circa 1850." Approximately 92″ x 100″. (Photo © 1989, Sotheby's, Inc.)

A simple calico border frames these disparate blocks so firmly and effectively. An interesting design exercise would be to cut a photocopy of this quilt into separate squares to see how they might be rearranged into a more dynamic set. But then we, who visualize our quilts hung at a quilt show or beaming from a book, would probably be trying to achieve a quite different aesthetic from this quilt's maker(s) who may just have asked that it look pretty on a bed. Note: The Odd Fellow star, five points on point, recurs elsewhere in similar heart-shaped boughs (block E-4).

Photo 4-11. Album Quilt, various signatures. 96" x 96". (Photo © 1989, Sotheby's, Inc.)

Three utterly elegant blocks in the ornate, more realistic style of classic Baltimore span the center of this quilt where they would be well-displayed on the proud owner's bed. The four outer corner blocks are repeated and lead the eye to the often-featured central nine blocks. Block B-1 with roses, hearts, and a Greek cross (or a plus sign?) causes one to pause. These crossed lines occur on several other Albums (see Photo 4-15, block C-2) and seem symbolically significant.[5] The border is of a less common botanical variety, being repeated discrete flower-and-leaf motifs rather than being depicted attached on a running vine.

Photo 4-12. Gorsuch Family Album. 103½" x 101". (Photo courtesy of America Hurrah Antiques, NYC)

This quilt's diagonal set is rare, though not unique, and is carefully worked out. The blocks are almost perfectly displayed if one imagines it covering the bed and draping over three sides. To have the half- and quarter-squares made to fit these shapes (rather than full blocks cut down) may be unusual in an appliqué Album, but may be more the norm in the Baltimore style. And this exquisite border, too, is rare with its broken garlands radiating from the corners. Only the quilt in Photo 4-27 has a running border which is in some way comparable to this in concept. This idea of a border which breaks at the corners or at the border centers makes for easy tailoring of the appliqué design for perfect fit.[6]

Photo 4-13. Album Quilt. 96¾" x 96¾". The Henry Francis du Pont Winterthur Museum, Winterthur, Delaware; gift of Miss Elizabeth Urian Lauer.

This is an intriguing quilt with a great deal of consistency. A bit crude by some Baltimore standards, it seems purposeful and the central monument would seem to tie it to the classic Albums. The featured central nine blocks seem here to be wreaths of oak, laurel, roses, and tulips (symbolic of Courage, Renown, and Love) surrounding a monument block where even a heart graces a nearby floral offering. Block C-5, a house surrounded by fully ten birds, appears portentous, but its message remains shuttered tight against our understanding. The border is a simple running vine of roses. And roses seem the most recurring botanical border motif in these quilts. The use of separate and different corners is of great interest in our study of borders. For while differing corners are only rarely found in the classic Baltimore Albums, the concept of individual corner patterns has great design potential for us. See quilts #7 and 8 in *Volume I*, and quilt #2 in *Baltimore Album Quilts — Historic Notes and Antique Patterns*.

Photo 4-14. Baltimore Album Quilt, inscribed, in part, *Baltimore*, and with multiple names. 97¾" x 97¼". Baltimore Museum of Art; gift of Dr. William Rush Dunton, Jr. BMA #1946.159.

Two blocks on this quilt have particularly appealing inscriptions: "Should I be parted far from thee / Look at this and think of me. / Mary Everist" (block C-4) and "May I twine a wreath for thee / Sacred to love and memory / Margaret Smith" (block E-4). Several other things are noteworthy about this quilt. One is that it has a good deal of buttonhole appliqué in it, even on blocks such as B-5 and D-2 where one might not expect it. Another is the relatively small finished block size (roughly 12½") and relatively wide border. The running feather border is both elegant and dramatic in its bright red against white. The outer edge of the feathers are reverse appliquéd, and the quill of the feather is a white soutache braid, the veining effected by embroidery.

Photo 4-15. Baltimore Album Quilt, inscribed in part, *Baltimore*, *1847*, and *1848*. 114⅝″ x 126½″. (Photo courtesy of the United Methodist Historical Society, Lovely Lane Museum)

On the two book blocks, Dr. Robert's name appears: "Find my lambs / Dr. Roberts / 1848 / Holy Bible / Caroline M. Mummy" (block D-2) and "To Dr. Roberts / Helen M. Pendleton" (block D-4). According to Dena Katzenberg, Reverend Dr. Roberts was a Methodist minister in the Baltimore circuit and 26 of the 36 names inscribed on the quilt were members of his religious classes.[7]

Magnificently large, this quilt is dramatic. With its irregular border corners and mixed-block motif sizes, it would seem to be a group effort and a grand Album selection. From blocks of exceptional simplicity to the most ornate Baltimorean *tours de force*, all here work amazingly well together. Visualizing this quilt as the top of the bed plus three sides, all to be read separately, it seems even more successfully composed. Care seems to have been taken to create a denser five-by-four block center bracketed by three relatively heavy blocks prominently centered above and below this. Anchoring this set are four strong corner blocks and a boldly vivacious four-stepped edging border (Pattern #25 in the pattern section).

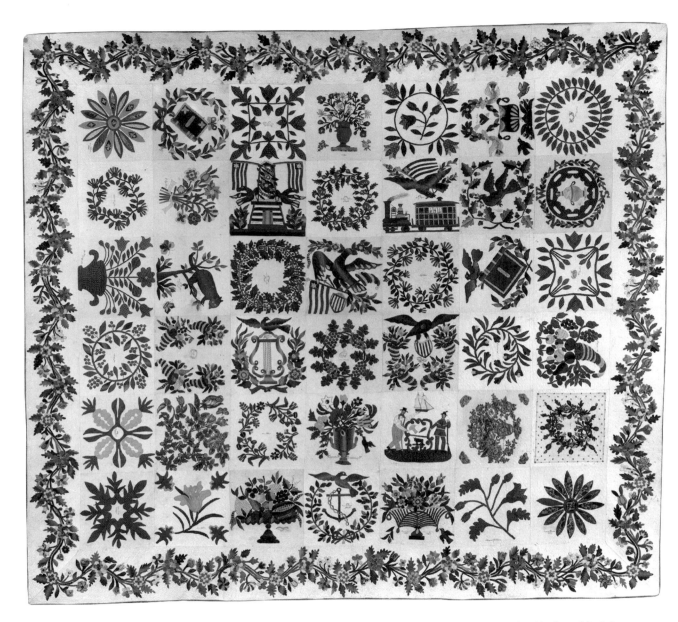

Photo 4-16. Baltimore Album Quilt, inscribed, in part, *Baltimore, 1846,* and *1847*. 106" x 120½". Baltimore Museum of Art; gift of Serena O'Laughlen Wagner. BMA #1988.206.

Dr. Dunton, in *Old Quilts* (p. 30), notes that this quilt is believed to have been made for Mr. Samuel Williams, a lay preacher and oyster dealer, by his religion class connected with the Exeter Street Methodist Church. A glorious Album, this one presents some of Baltimore's most popular block themes as well as those harder to find. Block C-1 has the ubiquitous square wreath with fleur-de-lis and rosebuds. It seems worth noting that the Masonic iconography which saw the square as "reminding us to regulate our conduct by principles of Morality" reflected popular sentiment as well. (Even to this day, we know a "square deal" when we see one.) Baltimore's War of 1812 monument seems depicted in block C-2. Two Great Star flags of the Union fly above it, their stars easily constructed of two overlapping triangles forming among other stars, the Masonic symbol, Solomon's Seal. Forming a Star of David as well, these two overlapped triangles are surely a most expeditious way for a quiltmaker to appliqué any star and so should be interpreted with caution.

In block G-2, a funerary urn has the appliquéd last name of Colonel William H. Watson, one of Baltimore's two most honored

Mexican War heroes. Interspersed with these block letters are fruited sprigs of what may be symbolic laurel, cherry, live oak, or acacia (a sign of Immortality). A railroad train, probably tokening the Baltimore & Ohio railroad, appears in block E-2. And while its inclusion is puzzling, the state seal of Delaware (adjacent to Maryland) seems represented in block E-5.

A Phrygian cap, symbol of freedom from slavery since pre-Roman times, denoted freedom from tyranny to Americans during the Revolutionary period. Here again it may symbolize freedom for fellow Americans in Texas from the tyranny of Mexico. Or, in block D-3, it may also suggest abolitionist sentiments. As for internal patterns created by the blocks themselves, is there a discernable Roman, or Christian, cross formed at the quilt's center? Tropical flora (Christmas cactus in block A-6, passion flowers in A-2 and E-3, and pineapples in A-5) may meld with exotic fauna in block B-3. For there, the tree-dweller resembles a koala bear more than a local Baltimore squirrel, symbolic of the virtue Thrift. And while this quilt as a whole has a group-made eclecticism, the border turns its corners so skillfully that it seems carefully drafted to fit. Even at that, many hands may have appliquéd it.

Photo 4-17. Album Quilt. 109" x 105". Museum of American Folk Art, New York; promised gift of Mr. and Mrs. James O. Keene.

Tropical allusions abound in this quilt, among them exotic birds (see the toucan in block B-4, and other bright species in blocks C-5, D-2, D-5, and E-3). Picture block A-1 shows a quite Baltimorean lady rowing in what could be a tropical lagoon.

The scene is set: shaded by a pagoda-like building amidst tropical flora, a clipper ship weighs anchor in the distance. Meanwhile, a similarly bonneted woman rows in the vicinity of a presumed Marylander who is happily waterfowling in the paired picture block. Around this fascinating Album assemblage is a lush rose-vine border whose prototype may be the chintz print of such a vine, shown in Photo 4-34. A small handful of classic Albums boast this opulent border, as though the original chintz had run out, leaving behind an image to be appliquéd. Another such border occurs in quilt #9 in the Color Section. Both that quilt and this one seem to show highly organized, intentional placement of the open wreath-shaped blocks. In both quilts, these form medallions, a square on point around the center; the baskets form a Greek cross around the central patriotic block. It seems noteworthy that in block C-3 in this quilt no Phrygian cap tops the symbolic freedom pole. (Some, though, have suggested that the strip-sewn cornucopias in these quilts may be presenting the same Phrygian cap in deeper disguise.)

Photo 4-18. Album Quilt. 104" x 110". (Photo © 1988, Sotheby's, Inc.)

Grid-quilted as so many of the most ornately Victorian of these quilts are, this one is very effectively bordered by a carefully drafted, simple, graphic rose vine. Although in classic Baltimore style, much of its fabric use is simpler than many in this ornate style, and the drafting of the familiar block images ranges from graceful to a touch awkward. It is educational, for example, to pick any block motif such as a diagonal cornucopia or the peacock in a bush (block D-5) and see how differently the same theme is portrayed throughout these Album Quilts.

What seems particularly sophisticated about this quilt is its set. As though learning from other quilts in the genre, several elements have been organized to create internal patterns within the block grid. Creating a strong diagonal motion to the center, the cornucopias point inward from each outer corner of the quilt.

Again, at the corner of the central nine blocks, four broken wreaths lead the eye inward, their heavier bases carefully placed at the outside corners so that their offerings spill through the openings towards the quilt's center. The pattern of open wreaths here again creates, though subtly, a square-on-point pattern. A stronger pattern is the Greek cross which radiates from the center block. The regular hills and valleys of the airy border both contain and keep in motion all this pleasing compositional pattern. This quilt is now in the collection of Ardis and Robert James.

Photo 4-19. "Appliqué Quilt, Mary Mannakee, Montgomery County, Maryland, circa 1850." 99½" x 99½". The Daughters of the American Revolution Museum; gift of Mrs. Benjamin Catching.

A "beyond" Baltimore quilt, this Montgomery County, Maryland, quilt is firmly in the mid-nineteenth-century Maryland Album Quilt tradition. A Greek-cross pattern radiates from the center block. Interestingly, the center block itself functions as a medallion, not because it is enlarged, but rather the opposite. Its scale is delicate and intricate and incorporates so much white space by comparison to the surrounding blocks. The same delight in line and in the variety of wreath shapes evinced by so many of these quilts is seen here. An airy, fruited vine border of grapes and apples breaks spontaneously at three of the four corners. A latticed circle knots the broken wreath of block A-3 and one wonders if it is just coincidence that features this same motif in the wreath in block E-4 of the quilt shown in Photo 4-13. Similarly, one must ask if the linked chain effect of the grapevine in block B-2 is meant to symbolize the Odd Fellow's chain of "Friendship, Truth, and Love." Its official representation as a three-linked chain is a relatively common occurrence in these quilts. Again, block E-3 is a recurring wreath shape which some quilt scholars call "the snail." Might it also be a mirrored "G," reflecting the Masonic hieroglyphic "G" for "Geometry" or "God"? It seems farfetched, but not, perhaps, out of character in these rather arcane-seeming quilts.

Photo 4-20. Album Quilt, attributed to Carrie Briggs, Melrose, Maryland. "Bride's Quilt, 1859." 92½" x 94". Newark Museum, Newark, N.J., Purchase 1967, Louis Bamberger Bequest Fund.

Another "beyond" Baltimore Maryland Album, this is one of several which sport enlarged Rose Wreath medallions. A particularly attractive style, two more of these will be featured in *Volume III*. (Those, however, are rectangular quilts which carry the wreath medallions one row above center.) Bold red wool stitching, daring and successful, embellishes many leaves and stems. And while the four carefully balanced vases may be original, the Rose of Sharon and Apple Wreaths beside them have often been seen before. The pinwheel-like placement of the smaller open wreaths gives a charming spinning motion to the whole quilt, a motion echoed by the likewise propeller-like crossed pine cone corner blocks. The complementary color scheme, too, almost entirely red, green, and white, adds to the vibrancy of the piece. All is kept in action by the undulating rose-vine border. While some of the previous rolling-vine-bordered quilts have white bindings, the strong colored binding on this one is dark and contains the quilt, producing a final and almost calming effect.

Photo 4-21. Album Quilt. Index of American Design, National Gallery of Art. #1943.8; NYC-te-108.

This quilt was recorded in the 1940s for the Index of American Design as a New York quilt. But it seems to be very much a mid-nineteenth-century Maryland style, and may have migrated north to New York in the hundred or so years since its making. You will recognize the block designs from Baltimore Albums and the border is a version of the simple running-rose-vine border so often seen.

Like the previous quilt, one can imagine this heirloom on a heavy-looking, high four-poster bed of the period, its sides draping over the edges to cover a trundle bed. The pillows were covered separately, perhaps with lace-edged cases. These two quilts are so similar in many respects, yet so different. Here the visual motion seems generated entirely by the fast-spinning medallion centered on a radiating star of hearts. As though to contain this passion, the border of Rose of Sharon, symbol of Wedded Love, holds close to the outer ring of blocks, which circle the shimmery center. As the view changes, one notices that the favorite square-wreathed block, the Fleur-de-Lis with Rosebuds, sits at each compass point of the center medallion, forms a Greek cross, and brings the quilt to a restless halt. Eight open wreaths, seemingly of cherry bunches, imply the kind of shorn-off, square-on-point medallion so successfully wrought in the Elizabeth Sliver quilt, shown in Photo 4-24. With so little recorded evidence, who can say who lead, who followed in the evolution of this shared quiltmaking tradition? What seems undeniable is that strong traditions, patterns, palettes, and passions were shared and influenced great numbers of good quiltmakers to classic heights.

Photo 4-22. Album Quilt, "1845-1850. Made by Elizabeth (Clarke) Hebb (1811-1873)" (*Old Line Traditions*, p. 17). (Photo courtesy of Mrs. Samuel Robert Garrabrant)

Discrete feather-plume motifs circle this quilt, to stop, momentarily, at the undulating edging border which frames each empty corner. The visual impact of this quilt is dynamic, the motion of the diagonal set clearly delineated by a chainlike sashing which darts around all the motifs, circling them back to a magnificent center. Full of symbols — hearts, cornucopias, arrows, harps, wreaths of laurel or live oak, chains, and stars — this quilt flirts with our understanding, teasing us, and ultimately eluding us.[8]

Photo 4-23. Album Quilt, from the collection of the Maryland Historical Society. Accession #57.80.2.

This quilt is in a rare set which incorporates open blocks of background fabric and a wide white border around the charming four-block medallion basket center. While I have not seen this quilt in person, piping occurs rarely as sashing, and may have been used here. In addition to the recognizable Baltimorean central medallion block, the pieced outer border of nested, framing strips is within the tradition of classic Baltimore Albums.

Photo 4-24. Baltimore Album Quilt, inscribed, in part (center medallion), *Bible / To / Miss Elizabeth Sliver / This is / Affections tribute Offering — / Presented By Father & Mother / To / Miss Elizabeth Sliver / Baltimore — 1849.* 104" x 104". Baltimore Museum of Art; gift of the Friends of the American Wing. BMA #1976.93.

A masterpiece of the genre, this quilt is artful both in concept and in execution. The evolving grid-based medallion tradition here explodes. Confined now to a squared ring around the enlarged Greek cross central medallion, the open wreaths frame this jewel-like center. One senses the culmination, here, of a shared presentation aesthetic. An evolution in this composition concept (the square-on-point medallion of open wreaths framing another central medallion) seems traceable. It develops from the dated 1847 quilt (Photo 4-34) where the open wreaths jump out at one a bit randomly, to the dated 1848 quilt (quilt #9 in the Color Section), where the open wreaths crisscross the quilt in every direction (but frame the central Greek cross with a square-on-point medal-lion), to this dated 1849 quilt where all blocks conspire to form a perfect whole. Such rapid and sophisticated design refinement implies intensive sharing of ideas and some common aesthetic ideal.[9] The significant nine-block center to the quilt still exists here, but it has taken on magnificent proportions with five of the nine blocks equal to 12 normal-size blocks. The four corner blocks of these nine are broken wreaths opening to the center and harboring magnificent exotic birds. Behind them cornucopias lead the eye inward from the quilt corners.

Photo 4-25. Album Quilt. 87¼" x 86¼". Smithsonian Institution Photo Catalog #E-363-155.

This quilt seems, on two counts, to be a fragmentary collection of blocks, finished into a quilt at a later date. First, the set seems off-center, and while the blocks are magnificently Baltimorean, the placement of the open wreath blocks seems not to follow the evolving pattern seen in similar completed quilts. Second, the quilt is, in part, machine quilted and the binding seems a bit wider than that in most of the classic quilts. These facts all hint at a partial quilt having been both set together and finished at some significant time beyond its blocks' making. It seems a shame, though, that this quilt was not completed, as presumably conceived into the 29-block set of the quilt in Photo 4-24, for example, since the blocks themselves are perfectly exquisite. The basket in block A-3, decorated with fancy feathered birds, and the garlanded eagle center block, are masterpieces of grace and intricacy, as elegant as any.

Photo 4-26. Baltimore Album Quilt, inscribed, in part (center medallion), *Presented to Capt. George W. Russell / By his Friends of Baltimore / August 23rd 1852.* 89¾" x 88¼". The Hooper, Strauss, Pell, and Kent Funds, Baltimore Museum of Art. BMA #1971.36.1.

Lovely, and less kinetic than the quilt in Photo 4-21, this quilt is quieter in fabric use as well. And while its flower-vined border is ornate, it is simpler than some and stately in the relaxed undulation of its hills and valleys. Like a telescoped version of the quilt shown in Photo 4-21, eight open wreaths frame the medallion center. Four well-composed cornucopias on point lead from the outer corners to the center, and each of their bouquets may contain something meaningful: a black-eyed Susan, perhaps, state flower of Maryland; acorns implying Longevity; a pineapple for "You are perfect" and Hospitality; and roses for Love. An anchor for Salvation, or to suggest a nautical theme, or as a fraternal symbol; the paddle-wheel steamer; baskets and bouquets of flowers; tropical birds and a wreath of Odd Fellow symbols topped by the All-Seeing Eye of God — all are blocks which must surely have pleased Captain Russell.

No freedom cap is included on the lovely central eagle block. That the Phrygian cap was on some of these quilts, but not on others, is understandable since even into the Civil War, Maryland (itself a slave state) remained severely divided internally on the slavery issue. Set squarely, block to block, this quilt has an open, airy beauty. A quilted running feather wreath frames the blocks and central medallion and can be seen here, most clearly with a magnifying glass.

Thirty stars surround the central eagle, a number to be taken seriously. For after the Flag Bill of 1818, each new state in the Union was to be represented on the nation's flag by an additional star. This dictum seems to have been taken seriously on the Album Quilts, not on the flags whose scale is too small, but within the configuration of patriotic symbols often around an eagle. Sometimes there are thirteen stars for the original Union (see Photo 4-3). But if there are more, count them and it may tell you something of the quilt's dates. Texas, a slave state, for example, became the twenty-eighth state on December 29, 1845. By law, the 28-star flag of the United States became official on the following Fourth of July, 1846. In an era where a well-wisher might make a flag by hand and the constellation's form was up to each designer (no law yet regulating placement), star composition was a significant issue.

You can see that the quiltmakers worked their stars in carefully, and treatment of the 30 stars here is skillful. Wisconsin joined the Union as the thirtieth state on May 29, 1848. Thus by July 4, 1849, the 30-star flag became official. By July 4, 1851, the required number of stars was increased to 31 to represent the statehood of California, a free state. Thus we might surmise that the central medallion of this quilt was designed with 1848's 30 state stars and appliquéd several years before the quilt was completed and presented to Captain Russell in 1852. That, in the meantime, the number of states had increased does not seem to have daunted the quilt's makers.

Before we leave this glorious patriotic block, let's take one last look. Of all the available graphic images of the day, our national emblem, the eagle, may have been among those nearest at hand. But what variety there is within these quilts in the drafting of eagle and flag, and in the fabric use! This eagle center medallion is spectacular. But look at that of the previous quilt, Photo 4-25. If two such beauties admit of comparison, that first rendering to my mind has even more grace and fluid majesty to it. Such subtle differences between the repeatedly rendered appliqué designs would seem to imply multiple needleartists working in a common style, a phenomenon with which we are all so very familiar.

Photo 4-27. Updegraf Album Quilt (quilt #8 in the Color Section) included here in a watercolor rendering to show the sashings and the quilting patterns. Index of American Design, National Gallery of Art. #1943.8; MD-te-14.

feathers' rhythm. Ardis James notes that this rhythmical scallop is led to by the narrowest yarn's-width of yellow piping, a skillful fillip of bright color just at the quilt's edge. Scalloped edgings are rare but not unique on Album Quilts of this period. This quilt is now in the collection of Ardis and Robert James.

This quilt is similar in set to those shown in Photos 4-20 and 4-26, but here white sashings between the blocks and two feather borders, one around the center medallion and one framing the quilt, give a wonderfully light and graceful look to the whole. The outer feather border is masterfully conceived. Broken at top, bottom, and at each corner, the rhythm of the running feather plume undulations changes, quickening and slowing to the eye, while the breaks in the plumes momentarily lead one beyond, and then back into the quilt. A lovely red scalloped edging echoes the

Photo 4-28. "Album Quilt, circa 1845. Made by a member of the LeCompte family." 88¼" x 86". Baltimore Museum of Art; gift of Mr. and Mrs. H. Lloyd LeCompte, Jr. BMA #1976.98.8.

From the background colored sashing of the last quilt, we come to this quilt, boldly sashed and bordered in strips of Turkey red. This is a simple and charming Album, but it points up the problem with the 16-block set (or any even-numbered set): there is no strong visual center. One solution is to combine the four central blocks into an enlarged medallion center as seen in several of the preceding quilts. Another is to fill the central blocks more fully than the surrounding blocks so that they read as a unit. An excellent example of this is quilt #2 in *Baltimore Album Quilts — Historic Notes and Antique Patterns.*

Photo 4-29. Album Quilt. Index of American Design, National Gallery of Art. #1943.8; MD-te-19.

The nine-block set, like all odd-numbered sets, has a clear visual center, making the organization of its blocks a simple affair. One could, for example, create a strong diagonal line moving from the outer corners and intersecting in the center block. Or one could emphasize each side center block, in addition to the very center block, thus making a Greek cross. Rather than changing the density or color or linear quality of the blocks, this quilt's maker has combined nine similarly balanced blocks and created a forceful design with the three-pieced sashings. Seemingly typical of the Maryland Albums, the vertical sashings read as all of one piece while the horizontal sashings appear to lie underneath them. Sometimes the sashings surround the blocks on all sides, as here. Sometimes there is no sashing where the outer blocks touch the border, as on the next quilt. Speaking of borders, this is a spontaneous looking charmer: a running vine with flowers and perhaps fruit, and weathervane-like birds.

Photo 4-30. "Album Quilt, circa 1845-1865. Made by Mary Ann Gray, Dorchester County, Maryland." 91½" x 88½". Baltimore Museum of Art; gift of Mr. and Mrs. James Frederick Andrews. BMA #1979.313.

The sashings and borders of this quilt appear to be pieced wide-based triangles rather than appliquéd ones. The quilt has a charming graphic consistency to it and its set seems very carefully thought out. The diagonal sprays to the left and right of the center face in opposite directions and it seems perfect so. One other quilt I've seen reminds me of these sashings and borders. It's a large Album in the Durner family of Maryland. In it, the sashings have facing stepped edgings, as does the border. What is intriguing is that, just as in this quilt, the edged strips seem made, then simply cut off to the size needed and sewn. Seemingly no attention was paid to how the designs on one piece intersect those of the next.

Photo 4-31. Baltimore Album Quilt inscribed, in part, *Baltimore May 8th, 1848* (block D-5), *BIBLE / Rev. Peter Wilson* (block A-3), and *Green Street Church* (block B-3). 79¾" x 97½". (shown sideways) The United Methodist Historical Society, Lovely Lane Museum; gift of Frank B. Mueller.

Wider than long, this quilt (here shown sideways) seems to have a nine-block focus centering on the church block, B-3. Some Al-

bum Quilts which are wider than long do seem to have these raised centers, as though they were meant to cover the bed to, but not over, the pillows. This raises the question of whether pillow shams may have been used. In *Old Quilts* (p. 127), Dr. Dunton describes one classic Album Quilt with a 36" by 69" pillow sham to go with it. The sham is centered on just one 17" block, a lyre-wreath block with the Baltimore monument to George Washington. A meandering vine border accented the top and bottom borders of the sham.

Photo 4-32. Baltimore Album Quilt inscribed, in part, *Baltimore May — 1848* and *1849*. 96¾" x 94⅛". Baltimore Museum of Art, William M. Ellicott Memorial Fund. BMA #1951.159.

Sashed and thus bordered by a printed floral stripe, this quilt seems poised in a careful balance of blocks. Seen from the foot of the bed, this set might be particularly pleasing with its regular pattern of circular shapes and bouquets. The center block is dramatic and draws the eye to it. While the open wreaths to the left and right of the center create a strong horizontal line, the vertical line from the center is not a strong design element although it is well-balanced. Block A-2 (Pattern #10) long intrigued me. It is rare, but not unique. The thought had occurred to me that it might have been a learning "sample" upon which the fine points of appliqué — points, curves, circles, straight thin stems — could easily be taught. Imagine my delight, then, when I found so similar a squared grapevine wreath block in the Oxford Female Seminary Quilt (Photo 4-6).

Photo 4-33. Album Quilt. 127½" x 142". Baltimore Museum of Art: gift of the Municipal Art Society. BMA #1946.101.

With this quilt being six blocks wide by five blocks deep, there is no strong visual center. Rather, the quilt is held together by the bold sashing which creates a pleasing grid of regular straight lines in marked contrast to the scallop of the hammock (or swag) and bow border. While space has allowed us to present only one of the Hammock and Bow borders (Pattern #23), this is a good place to make an observation about it. This quilt's border cuts across the quilt's corners at a diagonal, closing the quilt in. This is quite a different look from Pattern #23, seen *in situ* in quilt #16 in the Color Section or in quilt #6 in *Volume I*. In those quilts, the pattern dips deeply into the corner, opening it up in a joyous manner, rather than hemming it soberly in. Similarly, Pattern #22 from quilt #7 in *Volume I*, has a corner which I designed specifically to open the quilt up at its corners, a look which particularly appeals to me.

Photo 4-34. Baltimore Album Quilt inscribed, in part, *O may our hearts in tune be found / Like David's Harp of solemn sound / Presented to Mrs. Lipscomb by Mrs. L.F. Michalson / March 16th / Baltimore 1847 / Gen. Taylor Hero / of / Rio Grande* (on block B-1). 111¼" x 108½". The United Methodist Historical Society, Lovely Lane Museum.

This is an elegant quilt which blends three luxurious chintzes (two in the sashings, a third in the border) and a wealth of block and needlework styles. It has the aspect of a group-made quilt, and one might surmise that the group, or individuals in it, influenced or contributed needlework to other Album Quilts. The thread of a shared and evolving aesthetic seems to tie this quilt to other classic Baltimore Albums. Some simple clues to this — the use of the open wreaths, the basket-bordered center-block concept, and this rose-vine border (here in chintz and later in appliqué) — have already been pointed out along our tour.

The center block is unique and reflects exceptionally artistic use of heavy buttonholing, embroidery, sophisticated prints, and stuffed work. To myself, I call this style that of "the embroidery guild lady." For we do sense different styles in these quilts, and then, sometimes multiple variations on these styles. While there are yet more quilts to see at your leisure in the Color Section, our next chapter takes a more specific look at the kind of quiltmaking characteristics which each of us will have to consider when we take our Albums to completion.

[1]   Dunton, *Old Quilts*, p. 178.

[2]   Jeremy Cross, *The True Masonic Chart*, New Haven, 1824 , p. 23. One-page charts of fraternal symbols were used as teaching devices and widely disseminated during this period. At a time when fraternal orders were so popular, symbolic charts must have been a common graphic design source. Such motifs might have been used intentionally where small details distinguished one from another. For example, on Captain Russell's quilt (Photo 4-26) which includes an unequivocally Odd Fellow symbolic block, B-4, the anchor is shown differently, and is held by the favored linked chain rather than the rope-tied anchor of the Masons.

   Some quilts mix emblems of fraternal orders, the Odd Fellows and Masons being two popular ones. Others seem to have blocks that appear singleminded in their fraternal intent. Among the many things common to both Odd Fellows and Masons is the fact that they both consisted of steps, or degrees, to be learned and accomplished. One wonders if the attainment of degrees short of the highest might warrant a presentation quilt (or at least an honorific block)? Might the numbered steps in a stepped edging border, for example, reflect specific fraternal rank? The waters of antiquated symbolism are so murky (even for contemporary Masons to follow) that we may never have a firm answer. But if I, for instance, was moved to design a commemorative square (D-4 in quilt #7 in *Volume I*) when my son was elected to the Boy Scout's Order of the Arrow, then surely fraternal degrees may have similarly inspired Baltimore quiltmakers?

   Or, most understandable today, some emblems could have been used as modern quiltmakers use the Odd Fellow-originated symbol of the Heart and Hand. We think of it as just another pretty design with warm folk-art appeal, but with no personal attachment to the Odd Fellows, and probably no knowledge of its specific iconographic content. My own feeling, though, is that in Baltimore's Victorian heyday of symbolism, it's quite probable that iconographic vocabularies were used with fraternal intent.

[3]   Dena Katzenberg, *Baltimore Album Quilts*, Baltimore Museum of Art, Baltimore, Md., 1981.

[4]   Elly Sienkiewicz, *Spoken Without a Word*, Washington, D.C., 1983, p. 43.

[5]   Cross, *The True Masonic Chart*, shows these two crossed lines (like a plus sign) at the top of the Entered Apprentice Degree, Section first (p. 3). The verbal description, however, skips explanation of these symbols and goes right into the importance of the lambskin apron.

[6]   This quilt, which descended in a prominent Baltimore County family, is discussed in an article by Ricky Clark in *Quilt Digest*, 1987.

[7]   Katzenberg, *Baltimore Album Quilts*, p. 94.

[8]   Mrs. Garrabrant notes that this Album was made by a family ancestor, Elizabeth (Clarke) Hebb. Though her family became Catholic through a later marriage, the quiltmaker's family were originally all Episcopalians, and worshiped at St. George's Church, known as "Poplar Church" in Valley Lee, Maryland. Denominations seem worth noting when known, since non-Catholic secret societies were strictly proscribed for Catholics at midcentury. Not until the Knights of Columbus was founded in 1882 was there an acceptable alternative for all Catholics. At least one Catholic order though, was already established by 1836: The Ancient Order of Hibernians In America. Founded by Irish Catholics in New York City to preserve their Catholicism and nation-ality, its symbols include clasped hands, harp, shamrock, and a three-link chain: Friendship, Unity, and true Christian Charity. True, there is also an "unrescinded minute" on the Methodist conference minutes forbidding their clergy to join secret societies as well. But, noted Reverend Edwin Schell of the United Methodist Historical Society in a recent conversation, the mid-nineteenth-century church minutes also reveal numerous trials of ministers who seemingly had succumbed to the overwhelming popularity of these fraternal orders, and joined them despite that interdiction. In a recent conversation, Barbara Franco (author of several books on fraternal orders) noted that some members of churches, both Catholic and Protestant, joined fraternal orders because they provided insurance benefits. They joined despite Church disapproval.

[9]   Some Albums look much as many of us would present them today: a collection of blocks set in an appealing balance. But certain of the Baltimore Album Quilts, especially the more ornate, realistic Victorian ones, have a real sense of study, of pursuit of an ideal. One senses it in the blocks, too. Look at those wreaths — they are not just circles. They are lyres, or hearts, or crowns, or squares, or reversed G's, or half-circles, or facing half-circles, or facing or crossed sprays. It is as though the possibilities of line and form were being studied, savored, and pushed to the limit. In some of these quilts, one senses an almost passionate intent to organize the interior, to give it order, to create larger geometric designs out of the basic building block: the quilt square. Then, too, the forms this order takes are repeated over and over: crosses, crossed lines, circles, squares, and diamonds formed by squares on point.

   Sometimes one is struck in quilts with fraternal symbols, by the oddness of certain designs in the blocks. There are long, straight lines crossed in an "X" (sometimes graced with a leaf or bud at the end, but sometimes not). There are lines in a Greek cross, or crooked lines which Dr. Dunton describes as "like the peaks of houses." There are both wavy vines and snakelike lines. There are lots of squares; some are almost solid squares of fabric with a flower blooming off each side. There are sets of small circles — in specific and repeated numbers and colors. And then there are the variety of geometric shapes which comprise the "handles" which hang off many of the ornate, Victorian, red woven baskets: circles, ovals, squares, diamonds. It's all the stuff of geometry. *Webster's* defines geometry as "the branch of mathematics that deals with points, lines, planes, and solids, and examines their properties, measurement, and mutual relations in space." Was geometry primarily a design tool? A natural for the quiltmaker: a vocabulary of shapes and lines? Or was geometry almost a way of life, demonstrating, as *The True Masonic Chart* stated, "the more important truths about morality." According to the *Monitor*, one of a person's great duties was to act "upon the square, and doing unto [your neighbor] as you wish he should do unto you." And, "By [geometry] we may discover the power, the wisdom and the goodness of the Grand Artificer of the universe, and view with delight the proportions which connect this vast machine."

   Consider all the intentional dimensionality in the Baltimore Quilts: the layering, the stuffed appliqué and quilting, the clever use of textured prints, the passionate use of rainbow fabrics for contour. Might trying to portray "a solid — a figure of three dimensions" relate to this reverence for geometry, a key tenet in the Masonic imagery? Explaining the moral basis of geometry, *The True Masonic Chart* continues:

   "Geometry treats of the powers and properties of magnitudes in general, where length, breadth, and thickness, are considered, from a point to a line, from a line to a superficies, and from a superficies to a solid.

A point is a dimensionless figure; or an indivisible part of a space.

A line is a point continued, and a figure of one capacity, namely, length.

A superficies is a figure of two dimensions, namely length and breadth.

A solid is a figure of three dimensions, namely, length, breadth, and thickness....

Geometry, the first and noblest of sciences, is the basis on which the superstructure of masonry is erected. By geometry, we may curiously trace Nature through her various windings, to her most concealed recesses. By it, we may discover the power, the wisdom and the goodness of the Grand Artificer of the universe, and view with delight the proportions which connect this vast machine....

A survey of Nature, and the observations of her beautiful proportions, first determined man to imitate the divine plan, and study symmetry and order. This gave rise to societies, and birth to every useful art. The architect began to design; and the plans which he laid down, being improved by experience and time, have produced works which are the admiration of every age."

The True Masonic Chart, pp. 20, 31, and 32.

Barbara Franco, in *Masonic Symbolism in American Decorative Arts* (Lexington, Mass., Scottish Rite Masonic Museum and Library, 1976, p. 22), confirms the glorification of geometry: "The importance of science, and especially geometry and its initial letter "G" in the symbolism of Freemasonry, dates from the mid-18th century, the widespread interest in science had resulted in the popularization of scientific and mathematical terminology into everyday speech so that even common metaphors were drawn from the sciences. The French philosophers, Pascal and Fontanelle, both speak of the 'geometric spirit.' 'A work on ethics, politics, criticism,' Fontanelle tells us, '...is merely so much more beautiful and perfect if it is written in the geometric spirit.'"

It is irresistible to query whether these quiltmakers might not have seen the analogy between the quiltmaker with blocks seeking to build the perfect quilt, and the Masonic concept of living life "on the square," making of oneself a perfect block, so that Solomon's Temple, God's perfect plan, might be realized here on earth. Nothing in this quilt even overtly hints at such a notion. But Freemasonry and its philosophic constructs so imbued the decorative arts of the late eighteenth and early nineteenth centuries that the question deserves consideration. It seems to me that no Temple of Solomon built of blocks of stone could exceed the perfection of this quilt built of squares. In such a mood, one could see Odd Fellowdom in this quilt, as well. The three-linked chain of Friendship, Love, and Truth, might be masquerading as the triple bowknots tying so many garlands while the cornucopias (both an Odd Fellow symbol and the Masonic "Jewel of the Stewards of the Lodge"), offer their plenty and succor to those in need.

What seems undeniable is a fundamental similarity (both of symbolic imagery and of moral and religious tenor) between multiple mid-nineteenth-century associations. If this speculation touches on any element of truth, fraternal orders were more than just reflected by some of these quilts; they were a wellspring for them in some more substantial, more participatory way. And while it is tempting to spin out interpretations of what, to most of us, are foreign hieroglyphic tongues, it must be remembered that some Maryland quiltmakers, too, may have used these emblems as you and I will in our quilts. That is, for nonfraternal reasons of our own.

And what of final judgments on what symbolism antique Albums may have intended? Perhaps *Volume III* will help. There you'll see pictured the original nineteenth-century charts of key fraternal orders. With these in hand, you can ponder anew, and perhaps conclude, these hypothetical issues for yourself!

Figure 4-1. The Mosaic Pavement, a symbol of the Entered Apprentice Degree, from Jeremy Cross's 1824 *The True Masonic Chart*: " The Mosaic pavement is...the ground floor of King Solomon's temple [and is] emblematical of human life, checqured with good and evil; the beautiful border which surrounds it, those manifold blessings and comforts which surround us, and which we hope to enjoy by a faithful reliance on Divine Providence, which is hieroglyphically represented by the blazing star in the centre" (p.1). That the mosaic border is a running vine, looking wondrously quilt-borderlike, gives pause. The diamond pattern of the pavement is echoed in the Album Quilts by the diamond sashings, diamond quilting, and square-on-point medallion sets. Perhaps there is no import in this. But one can't but entertain the questions, "How serious were some of these quilts?" "How fraternal was their order?" (Photocopy courtesy of The Museum of Our National Heritage, Lexington, Massachusetts.)

Photo 5-1. The Little Mermaid of Copenhagen, appliquéd by Audrey Waite. Detail from the "Odense Album," quilt #17. Inkwork by Elly Sienkiewicz.

Chapter Five
Presentations:
Baltimore and Beyond

Like the packaged gift, festively wrapped and be-stowed with appropriate sentiment, the Album Quilt is inseparable from its presentation. After the fabrication and the inscribing of the blocks them-selves, the elements of the Album Quilt's presenta-tion are its set, its border, its quilting, and its binding. Crucial to the completion of the quilt, these elements are also dynamic design tools. For the most impressive of blocks loses a bit of its glory by nestling in an otherwise rather homely quilt. Conversely, the simplest of attractive blocks may sparkle and, by its contrast, lend drama to more complex blocks when both are part of a masterfully presented quilt. Accomplished presentation may include the most basic of sets and borders, or the most elaborate, if done with a sure sense of style.

Mid-nineteenth-century Maryland appliqué Al-bum blocks come down to us in all stages, from basted blocks to appliquéd but not-yet-set-together blocks, to tops (seemingly rare) or to tops quilted in this century, to quilts which appear to be incom-plete sets of blocks assembled in part by machine, decades after their making, to a complete set of 25 blocks set together and quilted with the help of a sewing machine. They come carefully designed so that their blocks self-border the quilt, or set together without borders or without sashing even, as though in a practical gesture to get a gifted or inherited set of blocks "made up" and quilted.

We can't speak definitively of the full extent of presentation elements in the Baltimore-style Albums since no one has yet seen all the Albums from that time and place. But we can make useful observations based on those we know of. By considering the op-tions illustrated by antique Albums, we can develop a connoisseur's eye for the genre, the better to create our own heirlooms in the best of this style. The fol-lowing discussion of presentation elements found in Baltimore-style Albums can only begin to answer the questions it asks. To it, add your own observations. For if we pool our insights, share our speculations, we will surely come to know much more.[1]

How many blocks are there in a Baltimore-style Album Quilt? From a minimum of four blocks up-wards, the most common set seems to be a square

one: five blocks wide by five blocks deep. Surely the quilt pictured in Plate 60 of *Old Quilts* must be close to the top block count. At 9' 6" x 9' 3", it is composed of one hundred six-inch blocks.

How are blocks set in the Baltimore-style Album Quilts? Blocks are set together with sashing strips between them, or set simply block next to block, without sashings. Blocks are set square or on the di-agonal. The blocks are almost all filled with an appliquéd (or, rarely, a pieced star) design. But at least one quilt (shown in Photo 4-23) is set with plain blocks alternating with its appliquéd blocks.

Where does the sashing occur? Some sashings run not only between all the blocks but line the inside of the border next to the outside row of blocks. Some do this on all sides, some do this just for the bottom and two side borders.

What is the size of the sashing? The size of the sashings vary. In my experience, it runs from as nar-row as a tiny piping width to over half the size of the block (as seen in Plate 60, *Old Quilts*, noted above). There the six-inch blocks sport sashings that appear to be roughly 3½" wide.

What do sashing strips look like? Sashing strips can be visually solid lines, or they may have corner blocks where they intersect. When they read as a solid line, the vertical sashings seem frequently to pass over the horizontal sashings, which appear to thread behind them. Sashing strips come in solid colors or in white background cloth. They may be made of informal calico or of a sophisticated im-ported chintz. Some are cut from printed stripes. The black/red/yellow striped prints of designs such as Greek key motifs or chains are particularly memorable. Sashing strips may be decorated with appliqués of botanical motifs or with geometric de-signs such as facing triangles and stepped edgings. They may even be pieced of something as simple as bordering strips of fabric.

How are medallions used? *Webster's* defines a medallion as "a large medal... an oval or circular

Photo 5-2. *Elly's Heart*, appliquéd and embellished with stuffed quilting by Judy Severson, 1989. Working a 12½" block pattern from *Spoken Without a Word* on a slightly larger square, Judy festoons it with exuberant plumage to elegant advantage. Years of embossing traditional quilting motifs into silk-screened prints as a professional printmaker have given Judy a flair for creating completely fresh and original patterns in this classic mode. This block may inspire those wishing an airier set to their quilt, or those seeking to incorporate smaller appliqué block motifs with larger ones.

design." In quilt parlance, a medallion has come to mean, in addition, an enlarged central design to a quilt. In the Album Quilts, medallions are usually in the center, but some circular wreathed medallions are set one row above the center. Again, while Baltimore-style medallions are usually enlarged, some same-size center blocks have the effect of a medallion because of their distinctiveness. (See the Mary Mannakee quilt, shown in Photo 4-19.) Seemingly, the most common enlarged medallion is the equivalent of four normal-size blocks in the same quilt.

Some medallions are formed by the design and/or color of equal-size blocks. See quilt #2 and quilt #9 in the Color Section. See *Volume I*, quilts #7 and #8, for an example of one block pattern repeated four times to effect a medallion center. Some 16-block-set and 36-block-set quilts have a four-block center. See Photos 4-20 and 4-26. When there is a center square equivalent to four blocks, it may be set either square or on point. There are multiple variations of a center medallion that's equivalent to four blocks and is bordered by double-sized blocks at its compass points (Photo 4-24). In the Philadelphia Museum of Art's Cynthia Ashworth Baltimore Album (*Volume III*), the center medallion (of a 49-block set) is the equivalent of nine blocks. It includes four borders of three designs. The "nine-block center" may occur visually on 25-block quilts, also. The arrangement of the center nine blocks, those which decorate the top of the bed, seem to have become a carefully worked out theme of great variety in the classic Baltimore Albums. The medallion center set, seen in Photo 4-23, on the other hand, is rare.

There are two versions of focus on the center which seem to be striven for repeatedly, with various degrees of success. One is the Greek cross which divides the quilt graphically into quadrants. Seemingly much rarer is the Roman cross, a semblance of which I've seen in just two quilts, one being quilt #3 in *Baltimore Album Quilts — Historic Notes and Antique Patterns*. On the other hand, the creation of a very large, square-on-point center medallion formed by an arrangement of same-size open-wreathed blocks seems an aesthetic ideal repeatedly striven for. This medallion forms a frame around the inner center which, itself, was often a carefully worked out Greek cross. (See quilts #9 and #14 in the Color Section and others in Chapter 4's Quilt Gallery.)

What do strips of framing borders look like?   Like sashings, borders come in a variety of fabrics, including chintz florals, border stripes, calicoes, and solid colors (including background colors). Some borders are pieced in long framing strips (see quilt #6 in the Color Section). Some are pieced of wide-based triangles, "flying geese style." At least one seems pieced of large wide-based triangles whose bases rest against the bound edge of the border and form lightning streaks as they are repeated on the border's inside edge. (See Photo 4-30.)

Often, borders are appliquéd. They may have geometric designs appliquéd, including triangles, stepped squares, or scallops. Or such representational motifs as feather plumes, or roses, rosebuds, leaves, and rose vines, may be appliquéd. They may also be of multifloral species, or fruited vines: grape or berries, sometimes mixed with flowers. Vines, a favorite design, are portrayed as single vines, or as multiple, intertwined vines, as straight vines, or as undulating vines.

Occasionally, individual flowers or leaves alone decorate a quilt's borders. In one quilt, oak leaves in a zigzag line march around its borders, stems facing towards its binding. In another, varied, realistic (as though traced from life) leaves adorn the border, perpendicular to the binding and pointing in towards the quilt. Again, varied leaves laid next to each other and facing all in one direction proceed in parallel diagonal tilts around yet a third Baltimore-style Album Quilt's border.

Multiple hammock (or swag) motifs embellish numbers of Album Quilt borders. Sometimes the swags are scalloped, sometimes they are simple, smooth moon crescents. Running swags may touch each other around the border. Sometimes they are joined by other motifs. Stars (linking moons), bows, tassels alone, tassels and birds, fleur-de-lis, roses, and peonies seem to be among these connectors. Of these, bows may be the most common.

What are border corners like? Border corners vary greatly, some being a continuation of the running border motif, some being of a quite different approach designed specifically to turn the corner. (For quilts with differing corners, see quilts #7 and #8 in *Volume I*, and quilt #2 in *Baltimore Album Quilts — Historic Notes and Antique Patterns*. I designed the corners to quilts #15 and #17 in the Color Section and in Color Plate #20 so that they open up the quilt at the corner rather than close the quilt in. Numbers of Baltimore-style quilt borders mismatch as they turn the corners. This might be evidence for a quilt having been a group, rather than an individual, undertaking.

What are Album Quilt bindings like? In general, the bindings are very narrow (roughly ¼" wide). These fabrics have been noted in Baltimore-style Album bindings: cotton, a woven striped binding, figured fabric, woven or braid bindings, velvet binding, and the quilt's backing fabric folded back, seamed, and brought to the front. The colors range from white to colored. The quilt in Photo 4-24, for example, is bound in an almost mustard-colored yellow, and some ornate quilts were bound in red velvet. White, red, and green, not surprisingly, seem to have been popular choices.

Some more unique and decorative bindings include binding with piping. Quilt #2 in *Baltimore Album Quilts — Historic Notes and Antique Patterns* has a narrow Turkey-red cotton piping, an eighth-inch or so of folded cloth nested in between the interior face of the quilt, and a narrow green binding that covers the piping's and the quilt's raw edges. Similarly, as noted, a tiny yellow piping lies between the quilt's edge and the scalloped edging of quilt #8 in the Color Section. Other unique edgings include scalloped edgings, (single or double layers of scallops), handmade lace fringe (see quilt #1, *Volume I*), and simple hand-tied fringe with wooden balls.

How are the Album Quilts quilted? All that I have seen are quilted in white thread. The quilting designs of these quilts seem to fall into four broad categories:

1. Those quilted in an overall pattern, often a fine diamond grid.

2. Those which serve almost as samplers of "filler quilting" patterns — those repeated patterns that fill in the background fabric behind the appliqués. Studied with a magnifying glass, these provide a wealth of ideas for overall quilting designs as well. Two excellent classic examples are quilt #2 in *Baltimore Album Quilts — Historic Notes and Antique Patterns* and the quilt shown in Photo 4-6. Susan Runge designed the quilting and quilted quilt #13 in the Color Section (in this volume) to skillfully combine filler quilting with custom designed quilting. The latter relates specifically to a given block's appliqué design and Susan has tailored her innovative designs to perfection.

3. Those which have an ornamental motif such as a feather plume running between the blocks. Or the motif may come at the intersections of the blocks and be more of a clustered pattern like a bouquet or a feathered, diamond-filled wheel or heart. Filler quilting would go behind these motifs. Borders, especially edging bordered ones with a long white space between usually have running motifs (feather plumes, grapevines) with filler quilting.

4. Those which are, themselves, albums of quilting. With each block quite differently quilted from the next, even in a white-to-white set, these are a delight to behold. Often the same sort of motifs which are appliquéd on the Album Quilts are quilted on to them.

There is a fair amount of stuffed quilting on some classic Albums. This seems quite in keeping with a fascination for incorporating the third dimension as well as with a clear desire to make the most elegant of quilts. Quilt #2 in *Baltimore Album Quilts — Historic Notes and Antique Patterns* has stuffed quilting and is certainly most elegant. Similarly, contemporary quiltmaker Judy Severson has a real genius for integrating flowing stuffed quilting designs with her appliqués and incorporates both needlearts as each block is made. (See Photo 5-2.) How? She draws the quilting design on tracing paper and lays it over the appliqué to see how it will look. Using the lightest of backing fabrics and wool rovings as a filler, she quilts the design, now drawn on the background of the block. When the quilting is finished, backing and rovings are trimmed right to the outside of the quilting. This stuffed quilting is an artful way of enlarging a smaller appliqué into a larger block.

Dogtooth Border Workshop

The dogtooth border (Averil Colby's term in *Patchwork*) is one of several examples of cutwork appliqué edging borders in quilts of the late eighteenth and nineteenth century. It is made up of strings of touching half-diamond triangles. That the dogtooth border was quite a popular Album Quilt border must have been due not only to its decorativeness, but also to the fact that it is fun, easy, and relatively quick to make by hand appliqué. One king-size dogtooth border strip took me just a day to make (with some sewing snatched during an evening Girl Scout meeting). Spin this fact out and you can see that a dramatic double dogtooth border for a large appliqué Album Quilt could take you just eight days or less to make!

As Lesson I in *Volume I* explains, the term "cutwork appliqué" means that the motif is not cut out until one section of it at a time is ready to be appliquéd. Some (though not all) traditional appliquéd dogtooth borders were made from whole strips of the appliqué fabric pinned or basted to the background border fabric (Figure 5-1A). Sometimes this strip was pieced once or twice along a border where one triangle ended and another began. The principle is that this strip is marked off at regular intervals, say 1", along its inward facing raw edge. At every other inch mark, you cut down 1½" on grain (Figure 5-1B). Cut just a few of the slashes at a time, cutting more slashes after you have appliquéd the preceding few down.

The size of the triangles can be adjusted to your taste and needs once the basic principle is understood. The principle is that the distance between the marks is equal, but the cut down is deeper (this frees the flaps on the right, then left side of the triangle to be folded under before being appliquéd down). You can comprehend this method very quickly if you simply accordion-fold a 2½" wide by 11" strip of paper by inches and tear 1½" down at every other inch. Starting at the right end, fold the flaps under to the uncut inch marks (Figure 5-1C).

Cut and mark the same size strip in fabric. Appliqué first the right side of a triangle, stopping ³⁄₁₆" from the top for seam allowance. Next fold under the left flap and appliqué the left side under (Figure 5-1C). Proceed this way across the whole strip. The flaps folded under each triangle remain there. This adds more strength to an appliqué border than tiny seam allowances would. And it was these remaining flaps which signalled to antique quilt restorer, Bette Faries, that this was how some of the old dogtooth borders were made.

All of the edging borders in the pattern section (Patterns #24 through #33) could be made by basting the colored fabric strip to the border and cutting and sewing a little bit of the design at the same time. To mark the fabric, for something other than the dogtooth border above, I would stack-cut the whole border out of freezer paper, and then iron it on as an appliqué guide. Accordian-fold the freezer paper. Mark one full unit of the border design and staple within the design to keep the layers from shifting as you cut. Open up the freezer paper and iron it to the right side of your fabric with a very hot, dry iron. Proceed as in Lesson 2 in *Volume I*. Beyond this being a very simple approach, cutting the border in freezer paper first will help you adjust the pattern to the exact length of your borders. May all your corner-turning, then, be more classically perfect, even, than those of bygone Baltimore!

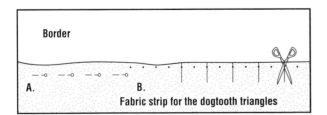

Figure 5-1A-B. How to appliqué a dogtooth border. A. The strip of fabric for the dogtooth triangle border is pinned the length of the background border fabric. B. Mark off equal intervals, say every inch. Mark only about 10" at a time along the dogtooth fabric strip. At every other mark, cut down 1½" on the grainline.

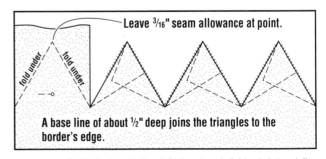

Figure 5-1C. C. Beginning at the right-hand end, fold a left-hand flap under and appliqué to the base of the triangle. Appliqué up the adjacent right-hand side to ³⁄₁₆" from the top and so on across the strip. Voila! Quick, easy, and template free!

---

[1] Joyce Gross, of the "Baltimore Album Quilts and Relatives" research project, has expressed willingness to receive any of our findings — photos of Baltimore-related quilts, added information, speculative insights — and to include it in the archives she, Cuesta Benberry, Kathlyn A. Ronsheimer, and their research associates are building and maintaining. Address: Baltimore Album Quilts and Relatives, Joyce Gross, 853 D Street, Petaluma, CA 94952. Please include a business-size SASE and your phone number.

Photo 6-1. "Basted Quilt Square of the City Springs." Attributed by her descendents to Mary Evans and recorded in the *Dunton Notebooks*. Believed to have been lost for decades, this block came to public notice again in Spring 1990 when Mary Evan's family sold it and the accompanying set of six blocks to the Maryland Historical Society in Baltimore. Notice the illustrations (trees, railings, fence) drawn in the center of the block even before it has been sewn. (Photo: The Baltimore Museum of Art: William R. Dunton, Jr., *Notebooks*)

The Color Section

Our Gallery tour of quilts, both "Baltimore" and "beyond" Baltimore, continues here. By visiting with these quilts, we'll better understand the issues of quilt presentation: how color affects the set, how color can help organize the blocks into interior pattern, and how the color of even the simplest border and binding affects the quilt. Our tour concludes in the late twentieth century amidst "beyond" Baltimore quilts and patterned blocks recently completed by our needleartists, the latter-day Good Ladies of Baltimore.

Quilt #1. Appliquéd Medallion Quilt.

"Priscilla Barnett Dodson, Cambridge, Maryland (1840-1845)." 101" x 101".
   Cotton with block- and roller-printed chintz appliqué. Philadelphia Museum of Art; gift of R. Ball Dodson.

Detail. Pattern in *Vol. II – Pattern Companion*

Detail (Block E-2).

This seems to be a rendering of the state seal of Texas whose origins go back to when Texas was a republic. The oak leaves and acorns of the seal represent the live oak, indigenous to Texas; the olive sprigs, Peace. The star is, of course, the Lone Star State, and the word "Texas" is worked beneath it in red wool. For historical notes on why there seems to have been such a close tie between Baltimore's quiltmakers and Texas, see "Part One: The Quiltmakers" in *Baltimore Album Quilts — Historic Notes and Antique Patterns.*

Quilt #2. Album Quilt, Baltimore, Maryland.

Six of the squares are signed or initialed. 117" x 109½". Gift of Mrs. John D. Rockefeller, Jr., Museum of Fine Arts, Houston, Texas. (Photo courtesy of the Museum of Fine Arts)

One senses a block design and style connection between this quilt and #4. Quilt #3 in the pattern companion to *Volume I* seems likewise to share the Texas theme. Note how the use of large blue elements seems to have established a Greek cross focus within the center nine blocks.

Quilt #3. Album Quilt descended in Baltimore-area family.

Inscribed with various names, initials, and the date *1846*. From a private collection.

A subtle central Greek cross is defined almost more by the squares which form its negative shape than by the airy red fruit and berry blocks which, extending from the bold blue eagle middle, form its positive. The repeated corner pineapple blocks help unify the quilt. Possibly significant is the fact that a similar pineapple block is in the quilt with the Watson memorial mentioned concerning quilt #3 in *Baltimore Album Quilts — Historic Notes and Antique Patterns*. And again in a sixteen-block Baltimore quilt (*Quilt Digest*, 1983, p. 36), a four-pineapple block version is repeated four times to create a central medallion.

Quilt #4. Baltimore Album Quilt.

Inscribed, in part, *Alice A. Ryder, April 1st, 1847, Baltimore, Md.* 122″ x 122″. Reproduced by permission of the American Museum in Britain, Bath, England.

Note how carrying the diamond sashing strips around the outermost edge of the blocks has created charming hearts at their intersections.

Quilt #5. Baltimore Album Quilt.

Inscribed, in part, *Baltimore, 1851*. From the collection of Woodlawn Plantation, a property of the National Trust for Historic Preservation.

Eagle-centered, red-white-and-blue bordered, this quilt seems to have patriotism and romance in the air. No fewer than eight pairs of birds (and one of butterflies!) nestle amid this quilt's blooms and the anchor block is inscribed, "In the Port of Bliss. Lizza Reynolds." Headed there on the prow of the *Alabama* is an inked couple. On shore, a dog, symbolizing Fidelity, Trustworthiness, and Watchfulness, stands under a tree from which quilted acorns (Longevity and Immortality) fall.

Quilt #6. Baltimore Album Quilt.

Inscribed, in part, *Hannah Foote, Baltimore, 1850*. 104" x 104". (Photo courtesy of America Hurrah Antiques, New York)

The stepped red calico border and narrowly sashed corner square set harmonize and enhance the blocks to perfection. Personally, I would move the central horizontal row one block to the left so that the two full-scene picture blocks framed the middle block. But that would put the gentleman in the central block of honor, rather than the lady. The figures are most intriguing, almost mysterious, and augment the quilt's interest and value.

Quilt #7. Album Quilt, variously inscribed.

Follett House Museum, Sandusky, Ohio. 112½" x 107". (Photo courtesy of Ricky Clark)

Here is another near-perfect Album presentation with its lush rose-vine border, echoed half-blocks at outer edge, dramatic pieced red-and-white striped sashing, "garden maze" set, and its blocks displayed on point. And then beyond this, what exquisite blocks!

Quilt #8. Baltimore Album Quilt.

Inscriptions include *Baltimore, The Album, presented to Mary Updegraf by H.H., 1850*, and *E Pluribus Unum.* 107" x 104". (Photo courtesy of Christie's)

An exceptionally beautiful and dramatic quilt whose uniqueness comes from the contrasting red reverse appliquéd feather borders which frame consistently lovely and ornate blocks. One straight feather border frames the center medallion, while the undulating outer border is particularly graceful and well-planned. Note: A similarly bordered Album Quilt appears in *Ho for California*.

Detail (left):
Block B-4.
No pattern.

Detail (right):
Block A-2.
No pattern.

Quilt #9. Baltimore Album Quilt.

Inscribed *To John and Rebecca Chamberlain, Baltimore, Maryland*, dated 1848. 108" x 108". (Photo © 1988 Sotheby's, Inc.)
   An opulently well-planned and executed quilt. Sophisticated composition and artful quilting enhance the near-perfect drafting, fabric use, and appliqué of the blocks and border.

Detail: Block E-2. No pattern.

Quilt #10. Baltimore-style Album Quilt.

Circa 1847-1850 (from Katzenberg's *Baltimore Album Quilts*, catalog #14.) Variously inscribed. (Photo courtesy of Hirschl & Adler Folk, NYC)
   Diverse gems of blocks comprise this brilliant Album. From appliquéd, inked, and watercolored figures, to layered, stuffed, ruched, and embroidered blossoms, to exquisite fabric use, this quilt comprises a treasure trove of the genre. Though simply made, its border provides a rich finish to the quilt.

Quilt #11. Album Quilt.

Inscribed, in part, with Numsen family names, and the date *1854*. 106½" x 122⅝". (Photo courtesy of Henry Francis du Pont Winterthur Museum)

Quilt #12. Baltimore-style Album Quilt.

Inscribed *Baltimore* and *1847*. 106" x 103". Gift of Nancy Rosenthal Millern, Herbert F. Johnson Museum of Art, Cornell University. (Photo courtesy of Herbert F. Johnson Museum)

An exuberant Album, this has the look of perhaps being designed, if not made, by one person. Eagle blocks were a repeated central block theme. Whether they contain the knitted striped Phrygian cap (a freed slave's cap) or not may indicate the maker's sympathies on whether new territories should enter the Union as slave or free states. Whatever one's leaning, no one wanted war. The country's motto, "E Pluribus Unum," so clearly penned on so many of these quilts, must have echoed fervent hopes as well as simply invoking tradition.

Detail: Block C-1.

"The Little Hunter," by Agnes M. Cook. 1985. Pattern appears in *Spoken Without a Word*.

Quilt #13. "More Maryland Flowers."

Group Quilt. 1984-1990. Designed by Elly Sienkiewicz, border appliquéd by Susan Alice Yanuz, quilting design and quilting by Susan Runge. Approximately 66" x 66". (Photo: S. Risedorph)

A wide border edged on both sides with the peony motif gives a bright, opulent look to this nine-block quilt. Despite its small number of 12½" blocks, this quilt just covers the top of a queen-size bed nicely with the addition of pillow shams. Use a magnifier to see Susan Runge's virtuoso "album of quilting," quilting designs which change from one block to another.

Quilt #14. "Baltimore Album Redone."

Group Quilt, by the East Bay Heritage Quilters led by Adele Ingraham. 1986-1988. 95½" x 95½". Pattern drafted by Adele Ingraham from the Metropolitan Museum of Art's poster of their classic Baltimore Album Quilt. (Photo courtesy of East Bay Heritage Quilters)

Quilt #15. Baltimore-style Album Quilt.

Made by Shizue Tsurumoto, Japan. 1989. Approximately 73" x 92". (Photo courtesy of S. Tsurumoto)

A meeting of East and West, old and new, this exquisite quilt uses some patterns from *Spoken Without a Word* and adds traditional Japanese motifs and other Album Quilt designs. Incorporating antique kimono fabric as it does, it is uniquely beautiful.

Quilt #16. "Petite Baltimore Album."

By Donna Collins. 1988-1989. 45" x 45". (Photo: S. Risedorph)

Donna designed and made this miniature Baltimore-style Album based on the patterns in *Spoken Without a Word* scaled down to a delicate six-inch block size. The quilt's set is exquisite and would be as beautiful full-size as it is in miniature — but perhaps not quite as astonishing!

Detail: Bottom center border medallion with inscription.
Pattern in *Vol. II – Pattern Companion*

Quilt #17 "Odense Album."

Group Quilt. Designed and inked by Elly Sienkiewicz. Border appliquéd by Albertine Veenstra. Audrey Waite made the sashings and set the quilt together; quilted by Mona Cumberledge. 1989-1990. (The block makers are listed in "Part Two: The Quiltmakers.) 70" x 70". (Photo by S. Risedorph)

Compare the evolution of the nine-block quilt set from quilt #13 to this one. Note the use of diagonal corner blocks in the quilt's interior and borders. Compare the border corners to quilt #7 in *Volume I*. The irregular meander of the grapevine border, inspired by the Updegraf quilt (quilt #8), creates an unexpected circle echoing the circular medallion center block.

1.

2.

1. *Goose Girl* (Pattern #15). Donna Collins, 1988.

2. *Rosebud Wreathed Heart* (Pattern #14). Jo Anne Parisi, 1989.

3. *Goose Girl Milking* (Pattern #8). Sally Glaze, 1990.

4. *The Sienkiewiczes at Home, with Acorn and Oak Leaf Frame* (Pattern #6). Elly Sienkiewicz, 1986. (Photo: © 1988 G. E. Garrison)

5. *Heart Medallion Frame (Pattern #7), with Katya and her Cats.* Elly Sienkiewicz, 1986. (Photo: © 1988 G. E. Garrison)

3.

4.

5.

6.

7.

8.

6. *Updegraf Basket, Book, and Bird* (Pattern #19). Detail from quilt #8. (Photo: Christie's)

7. *Bird in a Fruit Wreath* (Pattern #13). Ruth Meyers, 1990.

8. *Fleur-de-Lis III* (Pattern #5). Kathy Pease, 1990.

9. *Crossed Pine Cones and Rosebuds* (Pattern #3). Elly Sienkiewicz, 1987.

10. *Numsen Family Lyre* (Pattern #11). Elly Sienkiewicz, 1990.

9.

10.

11.

12.

11. *Joy Nichol's Peacock* (Pattern #18). Joy Nichols, 1987.

12. *Tropical Boating* (Pattern #17). Donna Collins, 1988.

13. *Squared Grapevine Wreath* (Pattern #10). Julie Hart, 1989.

14. *Joy Nichol's Rose of Sharon* (Pattern #4). Joy Nichols, 1987.

15. *Square Wreath with Fleur-de-Lis and Rosebuds* (Pattern #2). Elly Sienkiewicz, 1989.

13.

14.

15.

16.

17.

18.

16. *Wreath of Hearts II* (Pattern #12). Lisa De Bee Schiller, 1990.

17. *Jeanne's Grapevine Wreath* (Pattern #20). Jeanne Benson, 1984.

18. *Hearts and Hands in a Feather Wreath* (Pattern #9). Kathleen Reilly Mannix, 1990.

19. *Hans Christian Andersen's Danish Hearts* (Pattern #1). Eleanor Kay Green Hunzinger, 1989.

20. *Peony and Hammock Border* (Pattern #22). Zollalee Amos Gaylor, 1988.

19.

20.

Chapter Six
Dr. Dunton, Mary Evans, and the Baltimore Album Quilt Attributions

Photo 6-2. Dr. William Rush Dunton, Jr. (1868-1966), the first published expert on the Maryland Album Quilts. His *Notebooks* are the source for the name Mary Evans Ford in connection with the Baltimore Album Quilts. (Photo courtesy of the American Occupational Therapy Association)

In our journeys together, we have already touched on diverse potential influences on the Album Quilts. My intent has been to suggest new ways of looking at these quilts. Thus, ideally, two classic books in the field should also be read: William Dunton's *Old Quilts* and Dena Katzenberg's museum catalog, *Baltimore Album Quilts*. Everyone who becomes deeply involved in studying and writing about these quilts brings a certain mind-set and vision to them, a certain body of knowledge and research interests, and yes, certain artistic preferences. Only multiple voices will help us fully appreciate and understand the Album Quilt genre in all its diversity. And no single explanation can enlighten us fully on so complex and widespread a cultural phenomenon as these mid-nineteenth-century Album Quilts.

When *Volume I* was written in 1988, it seemed impossible to write about Baltimore Album Quilts without considering Mary Evans. Dena Katzenberg in *Baltimore Album Quilts* attributes numbers of these quilts to this woman about whom so little, really, is known. The feeling growing among many contemporary Album Quilt makers was that no one person, alone, could have worked so fast, with such diversity of design and with such intricacies of embellishment, and at such a sustained pace as to have created so many masterpieces in a short period of time. My fascination with the question of her authorship consumed the early half of 1989. And because the Mary Evans theory has caught the imaginations of so many, it seems important to share something of that winter's work here.[1]

First, who was Dr. Dunton and how is he connected to the Mary Evans attribution? Dr. William

Rush Dunton, Jr. (1868-1966), whose unpublished *Notebooks* are the original source for the name Mary Evans (married name, Ford), was an Album Quilt scholar. *The National Cyclopedia of American Biography* devotes a half-page to Dr. Dunton, highlighting his role as a psychiatrist and one of the founding fathers of occupational therapy. Only a few lines in that biography hint at his love for needlework and quilts. One such clue is his belief that quiltmaking would restore a positive state of mind to "nervous ladies"; another, the fact that one of his contributions to medicine was the introduction of "white duck" fabric for use in interns' uniforms; and finally, the inclusion of the phrase "old quilts" in a list of his hobbies. By contrast, it is delightfully clear from the record he left behind that Dr. Dunton's quilt hobby was nothing less than an abiding passion and it is this "quilt record" which is of particular interest to us as quiltmakers.

Dr. Dunton felt the data he had researched and collected on the old quilts of Maryland and surrounding regions was so important that he self-published 2,000 copies of *Old Quilts* in 1946. Now a rare collector's item, that book was the first study to include in detail what we now call, loosely, the Baltimore Album Quilts. In addition to *Old Quilts*, Dunton left files, over a dozen "notebooks" (scrapbook albums, correspondence, news clippings, articles written by him, photos), and a partial manuscript for a book in progress, a "Dictionary of Quilt Names and Patterns." Now collectively called the William Rush Dunton, Jr., *Notebooks*, and housed in the Baltimore Museum of Art, these uncataloged papers are a treasure trove of quilt history. Dunton corresponded with such quilt luminaries as Marie Webster, Florence Peto, Carlie Sexton, Phoebe Edwards, and many others, whose names are no longer familiar to most of us. Included are Dunton's letters to batting companies, bed manufacturers, and an indelible ink company — all seeking answers to questions raised by these old quilts.

Perhaps Dunton discussed authorship of the Baltimore Album Quilts with Florence Peto, for in her 1939 book she wrote, "One wonders if there might not have been professional needlewomen in Baltimore and possibly other localities who specialized in fine quilts and spreads for bridal trousseau. There seems little evidence to support my idea except the character of the workmanship on the quilts." Dr. Dunton was still pondering the same question when he published his book in 1946.[2]

"I have a theory which cannot be proved," wrote the psychiatrist cum quilt expert in *Old Quilts*. "An artist...made her living by making [Baltimore Album] quilts... [and she] acquired considerable local fame." This modest statement doesn't sound like the stuff of which myths are made, but it may have happened. Mary who? Fewer people would ask that question in 1989 than in 1988, for the answer had been streamlined and packaged for popular consumption. Two books published in 1974 first tentatively suggested that Mary Evans might be just that needleartist whom Dr. Dunton sought. Fifteen years later, cautious speculation had given way to confident assertion. The word was out. Mary Evans was a "master quiltmaker," the "first professional quiltmaker."[3] Mary Evans supplied "prefabricated blocks for which she received payment" and signed "those blocks in a standardized script with their donors' names."[4] Mary Evans seemed to be the hottest-selling quiltmaker of the mid-nineteenth century. Is it true? Did she really make — in roughly a half-dozen years — the more than a dozen quilts now popularly attributed to her? Let's look at how that assumption may have affected quilt prices in recent years.

Record quilt prices of six years ago look like bargains today as Americana prices escalate. On January 21,1989, a Baltimore Album Quilt dated 1850 and described as "the work of Mary Evans...commissioned as a gift for Mary Updegraf by her wealthy family"[5] sold at Christie's Auction House in New York for $132,000. (The same quilt appeared on the cover of Dutton's *Quilt Engagement Calendar 1984*.) Thomas K. Woodard (owner of Thomas K. Woodard: American Antiques and Quilts) told me that it had sold at the time of that publication for $26,000, so the 1989 sale shows more than a five-fold increase in just five years. At Sotheby's January 1987 Americana auction, another classic Baltimore Album Quilt sold for $176,000, and, according to its buyer, Frank J. Miele of Hirschl & Adler Folk, resold the same evening for "at least $200,000." In 1988, a classic Baltimore Album Quilt dated 1848 and inscribed "To John and Rebecca Chamberlain," with the maker listed as "probably Mary Evans"[6] sold for $110,000. In 1972, the *National Antiques Review* had pictured that same quilt and reported that at the Pennypacker Auction House in Kenhorst, Pennsylvania, "it surpassed everything else in beauty, interest, and price — $3,800."[7] In sixteen years, then, this classic Balti-

more Album Quilt had increased in price roughly 3,000%.

January 21, 1989, was a Saturday quilt shoppers will remember. It was fur weather and antiques were in the air. Those who made the Christie's/Sotheby's/Winter Antiques Show[8] circuit quickly caught a theme: all three were offering Baltimore Album Quilts attributed to Mary Evans. "It's her! It's another quilt by Mary Evans!" I heard exclaimed for the third time. I had been standing awhile at the top of Sotheby's main staircase, making notes on the quilt "attributed to Mary Evans, Baltimore, Maryland, mid-19th Century."[9] When the young man added "It's not as nice as the one that sold at Christie's this morning," I couldn't refrain from asking what the quilt at Christie's was like. He and his friend shared their catalog. The quilt in question was quilt #8 in the Color Section of this volume. "And the one at the Winter Antiques Show?" I asked. "Oh, it was much fancier than this one, but here, take this extra ticket, we have to catch our plane." I had a train to catch, too, but there would be other trains.

My stopover at the Winter Antiques Show was worth it. I recognized the quilt in America Hurrah's booth from the *Quilt Engagement Calendar 1989* (see Photo 4-12), where its caption reads: "inscribed Ellenor [sic] and Elizabeth A. Gorsuch, ca. 1840 ... many blocks ... may confidently be attributed to the hand of Mary Evans." (Birth dates for Mary Evans are given variously as 1829 or 1830, making her ten or eleven years old in 1840. It is hard to imagine so young a child having made a piece of needleart of this magnitude.) The Gorsuch Album Quilt was labeled at the show as having descended in a Baltimore County family with the date now changed to "circa 1845." Such provenance alone makes it very valuable even without further specific attribution. "Sold," proprietor Joel Kopp replied to my fellow customer's query, "for a high five-figure price."

The three Baltimore Album Quilts offered that Saturday had all been advertised in print as "attributed to Mary Evans" or "made by Mary Evans" — yet her name appeared on none of them. What is the origin of this attribution? The name "Mary Evans" was connected to the Baltimore Album Quilts in the mid-twentieth century by quilt expert Dr. Dunton with his "theory which cannot be proved," and despite subsequent research, it remains unproven today. Her name doesn't appear on any Baltimore Album Quilts that we know of, yet this attribution to Mary Evans, is confidently asserted in the marketing of these quilts. Thus, while the popularity of quilts as collectors' items is now well established, quilt authentication standards in the marketplace need to catch up.

Attribution to Mary Evans (for one unappliquéd block only) seems to have begun with a manuscript dated 1938 in the Dunton *Notebooks*. In 1974, Patsy and Myron Orlofsky[10] and Marilyn Bordes[11] published the first tentative references to Mary Evans by name. They cite (either in person or in print) the Dunton *Notebooks* as their source. I went to the Baltimore Museum of Art to read for myself the reference to Mary Evans in these fragile old documents. The *Notebooks* convey in Volume VIII that Evans Bramble (identified by Dena Katzenberg in *Baltimore Album Quilts* as Arthur Evans Bramble, Mary Evans's great-nephew) brought Dr. Dunton a set of seven quilt blocks.[12] One, a central medallion block depicting the City Springs, Dunton records through a photograph and a notation as "made by Miss Ford" (Mary Evans's married name). (See Photo 6-1.) That attribution is contained in a seven-page description of this set of blocks. The sophisticated City Springs block, which is only basted, is in the very realistic, decorative, Victorian-style uniquely associated with Baltimore. By virtue of its being connected to Mary Evans through the *Notebooks*, this block's style, one that weaves through the Baltimore Album Quilts, has come increasingly to be thought of as Mary Evans's style.

If made during the heyday of the Baltimore Album Quilts, that City Springs block would have been begun one hundred or so years before being brought to Dr. Dunton. We won't ever know exactly what phrasing Mr. Bramble used to attribute this work to his great-aunt, but the passing of some one hundred years, one suspects, might cloud the Evanses' recollection of exactly what Great-aunt Mary's role in that block had been. Did Mary Evans design the elegant City Springs block herself? Or did she cut it out of fabric from someone else's design? Was it her own work in this block at all, or had someone else cut and basted the motifs for Mary Evans to finish?[13]

Some of the other blocks in the set are already signed, though none "Mary Evans," and the needlework, in Dunton's words, varies in quality from "quite beautiful" to "rather crude." Might this have been a group-made presentation quilt with young Mary helping with the sewing? Or had these blocks come in from friends as contributions to Mary's own, never finished, Album Quilt? Was she, in fact, a professional seamstress or simply the designated sewer who had been brought the basted center block to appliqué and the other blocks to set together when all were finished? In any one of these suggested roles, the block connected to her might have descended in her family as "the work of" Great-aunt Mary. In the end, while the City Springs block does clearly reflect a design style, we don't know for sure whether this style is Mary Evans's or

that of another. And if it is Mary Evans's, we don't know whether she originated the style or was one of a number of people working in that style. This block was brought to Dunton with two completed quilts, both rather mundane square-patch variations. We are not told if they, too, were the work of Mr. Bramble's great-aunt, Mary Evans. What can safely be said is that, photographed in black and white, at least, they don't show the distinctive spark of an artist.

Katzenberg gives the birth/death dates for Mary Evans as 1829-1916 and cites the services in her book of Robert Barnes, genealogist. Dunton records what are presumably Evans Bramble's dates for Mary of 1830-1928. If Katzenberg is right, then Great-nephew Bramble is wrong at least on this item in his facts about the block and its maker. One must also question why, if Mary were either an extraordinary needleartist or a prolific professional quiltmaker, her family seems to have had so little evidence about her quiltmaking activities. Mary Evans lived to be 87 years old, by Katzenberg's dates, or 98 years old, by Evans Bramble's dates. By both reckonings, she lived right into those early twentieth-century decades when Dunton himself was actively researching quilts. Yet seemingly the only evidence of quiltmaking activity to come out of all those years of adult life is one unfinished block said to have been begun when she was 20.

While he records this block as made by "Miss Ford," William Dunton does not once suggest that she might be "the artist" whom he seeks as the maker of other Baltimore Album Quilts. In writing about this set of blocks, he does reiterate his alternative theory that there may have been shops which sold patterns for these unusual designs. And what of Dunton's opinion of the possibility that Mary Evans may have been the artist in his theory? After having written about this "entertaining" set of blocks and Miss Ford in 1938, he left them and her out completely when, eight years later in 1946, he published his magnum opus, *Old Quilts*. Then again when, towards the end of his life, he compiled the files which "should go with the albums to the Baltimore Museum of Art...where [they] will be accessible to anyone who may be interested," he makes no mention of Mary Evans in all of his alphabetized letter-file boxes. He does, however, refer back once in those files to the City Springs block, though with no attribution to Mary Evans. In the manuscript section on naturalistic appliqué, for his never-published quilt dictionary, he wrote, "There was also a large block made for a quilt which was never completed which showed a familiar sheltering, one of the City Springs. Unfortunately during the absence of the owners, their house was broken into and this fine piece has been lost. Fortunately I had secured a photograph of it previously." Not until 1990 did news break that the descendents of Mary Evans had inherited the Springs block, and indeed the whole set of seven blocks, and had sold it that spring to the Maryland Historical Society in Baltimore.

Writing about the quilt dated 1850 and made for Dr. John P. MacKenzie in that ornate, Victorian style which we now identify with Baltimore, Dr. Dunton conjectured, "It is unfortunate that the maker of such a masterpiece of needlecraft should be unknown....Evidently the woman was an artist as is shown by her sense of form and color and probably in a later period would have been a painter. I have a theory which cannot be proved but which seems plausible to me, and that is, that she made her living by making quilts." Manifesting that he was still looking for that "artist," despite having been brought "the work of Mary Evans" some eight years earlier, he immediately follows the 1946 presentation of his theory with an open invitation for help: "It is hoped that old letters or other records will give information as to the name and personality of this wonderful needlewoman."[14] Further on he continued, "I am of the opinion that these designs were probably sold at shops or that they were the work of one woman who practiced quiltmaking as a profession."[15]

In 1974, almost thirty years after the publication of *Old Quilts*, the Orlofskys wrote that "enterprising seamstresses may have supplied quilt block patterns much as needlepoint experts today. It is also believed that a professional needlewoman living in Baltimore, Mary Evans Ford, may have produced a number of these beautiful Baltimore Album quilts, and as many as twenty-six."[16]

Seven years later in the Baltimore Museum of Art's catalog to the 1980-1982 traveling exhibition, *Baltimore Album Quilts*, Dena Katzenberg again presented the theory of Mary Evans's role in the Baltimore Album Quilts.

An unfinished quilt block, one of a set of seven with pencil lines, and basted appliqués, was brought to the attention of the quilt expert, Dr. William Dunton, by Arthur Evans Bramble. Bramble informed Dr. Dunton that the blocks were the work of his great-aunt, Mary Evans....This piece established some of the hallmarks of Mary Evan's works: triple bowknots, prominent white roses, figures with inked features, the use of rainbow fabrics to indicate contour, a sure sense of formal design, and compositional skill. Such careful elegant work on so many quilts leads to the conclusion that a professional quiltmaker was at work. The author has identified over a dozen quilts which she considers to be the sole work of Mary Evans, and numerous individual blocks on other quilts.[17]

Katzenberg herself, later in her book, is somewhat more tentative about Mary Evan's possible authorship: "There is some reason to believe that the artist of the most proficient work on the Baltimore Album quilts can be identified as Mary Evans."[18] Ms. Katzenberg's research has unearthed a rich trove of information pertinent to these quilts, but on the attribution to Mary Evans it seems not to be conclusive.

In 1987, Schnuppe Von Gwinner's book, *The History of the Patchwork Quilt*, was published. In the chapter on "Friendship and Album Quilts" it states, "Mary Evans and Achsa [sic] Godwin [sic] Wilkins of Baltimore were so talented and famous that they sewed whole album quilts and also individual blocks for others commercially."[19] This statement is not footnoted. Dunton is not listed in the bibliography but Katzenberg's *Baltimore Album Quilts* is included. *Baltimore Album Quilts* cites Dunton's *Old Quilts* for four out of six of Katzenberg's notes on Achsah Goodwin Wilkins (1775-1854), including the quote referring to her quiltmaking activity. Katzenberg clearly couches the connection of Wilkins to the Baltimore Album Quilts as her own "hypothesis."[20] Referring back to Dunton as the original source, we find there a quoted reference about Achsah Wilkins by one of her daughters, Mrs. Allen Bowie Davis.[21] But we also find Dunton's forthright statement, "There is no real proof that she [Wilkins] was the maker [of the series of chintz medallion quilts]....It would be pleasant if family tradition held more about the personality of this lady and her habits, especially those connected with her quilt industry, and how she acquired such beautiful chintz patterns for her materials. Perhaps some day one of the old trunks, now in attics, will be cleared and a diary or letters will be found which will give us this information."[22]

Also in 1987, the book *Hearts and Hands* included a statement of Mary Evans's role in these quilts: "We now know from the meticulous research of Dena Katzenberg that many Baltimore album quilts were made with some or all of the blocks designed by professional quiltmaker Mary Evans....The entrance of a professional like Baltimore resident Mary Evans into quiltmaking was a new departure....Mary Evans's procedure [was]...supplying prefabricated blocks for which she received payment (and also...signing those blocks in a standardized script with their donors' names)."[23]

By 1987, had new evidence turned up to confirm these conclusions? The footnote to the above quotation refers the reader back to the pages in *Baltimore Album Quilts* from which we have already quoted.[24]

Yet it is these subtle shifts of theory into fact that may have set the tone for the confident attribution in January 1989 of Baltimore-style Album Quilts to Mary Evans. An evolution from hypothesis to postulate in the marketplace, parallel to that in the scholarship, is manifested by the repetition of the same set of three paragraphs describing Mary Evans's work being repeated in three consecutive Sotheby catalogs for three different Album Quilts. Sotheby's credits Julie Silber, co-author of *Hearts and Hands*, for those paragraphs. Those excerpts reflect that book's confident view of Mary Evan's role in the authorship of Baltimore Album Quilts. (The actual attributions for these three quilts and their publication sequence are as follows: sale #5680, lot #1463 (January 1988) "Probably Mary Evans"; sale #5755, lot #143 (October 1988) no specific attribution is given in the notation "Variously signed," but the bulk of this quilt's description consists of discussion of Mary Evans; and, finally, for sale #5810, lot #1106 (January 1989) the stated authorship is "attributed to Mary Evans.")

Attribution to Mary Evans became markedly less ambiguous in the early winter of 1989, following a slower quilt market in the fall of 1988. "Quiet Time for Quilts, Caused by Discriminating Buyers Who Will Settle Only for the Best," pronounced the title of an article by Frank Donegan in *Americana Magazine*. He quoted Nancy Druckman, Sotheby's folk-art specialist as saying, "We're finding out that these [Baltimore Album Quilts] may not be as rare as we thought. A couple of $100,000 prices show you just how un-rare something is."[25] Perhaps the irony of the story is that to this day the record high-selling quilt, a Baltimore Album Quilt (quilt #2 in *Volume I*) and sold by Sotheby's in January 1987, was not attributed to Mary Evans. Her name was not even mentioned in the catalog description although, by January 1989 standards, much of that quilt could have been attributed to her hand. The majority of its blocks are in the ornate, highly realistic, Victorian style associated with her name.

The increasing confidence of Mary Evans attributions for two of the three quilts offered for sale on January 21, 1989, has left a paper trail. From the 1988 publication of Dutton's *Quilt Engagement Calendar 1989* to January 1989, the wording changed on the attribution of the Gorsuch Baltimore Album Quilt: "Many blocks...may confidently be attributed to the hand of Mary Evans"[26] became "Baltimore Album Quilt, made by the master American Quiltmaker, Mary Evans, circa 1845, for Eleanor [sic] Gorsuch, Baltimore County, Maryland."[27]

Similarly with the Updegraf Album Quilt offered by Christie's, the attribution to Mary Evans had also metamorphosed, though a bit more slowly. In the *Quilt Engagement Calendar 1984*, a description credited to Thomas K. Woodard concerning the Updegraf quilt reads, "It is quite probable that the quilt is the work of Mary Evans." Some five years later, in the *New York Times*, Rita Reif wrote, "An 1850 Baltimore Album Quilt by Mary Evans, the master quilt maker who created pieced coverlets with patriotic and nostalgic references between 1840 and 1860 is to be auctioned at Christie's."[28] Her article continues, "'She was the first professional quilt maker,' said Jan Wurtzburger, a Christie's folk-art specialist. 'This quilt has all the special hallmarks of her style — the triple bow knot, reticulated baskets, white appliquéd roses, intricate stitching and a careful and deliberate selection of the squares.'" Note the reference to Mary Evan's intricate stitching and reticulated baskets, though neither appear in the City Springs block.

Based on my own experience in examining needlework closely, I'd say the three quilts attributed to Mary Evans and offered for sale in New York that January Saturday contained work by at least three different women. What is the same in all three quilts is the dominant pattern style: ornate, quite realistic, decorative, Victorian. But one style does not mean just one maker. What of the evidence from quilts done in the classic Baltimore Album style today? Some are as breathtaking in the mimicked fabric use and refined needlework as the vintage quilts they replicate. What, beyond age and period fabric, would distinguish these similarly-styled quilts from the originals? Would we always be able to assess whether one person or more than one made a quilt of a uniform style? Again, the present aids our understanding of the past. In the March 1989 issue of *Country Living Magazine*, Mary Roby reviewed the replica[29] (quilt #14 in the Color Section) of the Metropolitan's Baltimore Album Quilt, circa 1849, attributed in Katzenberg's *Baltimore Album Quilts* to Mary Evans. "It took a year for 30 quilters to complete...the quilt's top;...[more than] six women completed the quilting in five months." And what was the quality of the work having been done by so many people? "Meticulous uniform quality," the article concludes.

Are there criteria which could help us understand more about who was working in the uniquely Victorian Baltimorean style? I believe so, but even such quantifiable factors as type and length of stitch will not identify a particular quiltmaker beyond all doubt. It's a bit like identifying handwriting done in an archaic calligraphic script on fabric. Hundreds of specimens may be separable into a few gross and inconclusive categories. But studying objective criteria may suggest an answer to the question of one or multiple sewers, for example, of blocks in which fabric and design are similar. And if sufficient data is gathered, a confluence of characteristics may point to a given hand.

Katzenberg concludes, "Such careful elegant work on so many quilts leads to the conclusion that a professional quiltmaker was at work." Yet it is just that "conclusion" that has raised questions among scholars and quiltmakers. That Mary Evans made so many Album Quilts from start to finish just isn't consistent with what contemporary quiltmakers are learning about them. Many of us are making quilts in the classic Baltimore Album style, reproducing classic patterns or designing our own in this style, and keeping track of the hours we spend. I recorded about 50 sewing hours for an ornate Victorian style block like "Silhouette Wreath,"[30] and a bit less for the simpler "Ruched Rose Lyre." Professional quiltmaker Donna Collins, the speediest appliqué artist I know, reproduced the classic Baltimore Album Quilt block portrait of a manor house (Color Plate 1) in about 40 sewing hours, while Cathy Berry reported up to 60 hours to appliqué an intricate block such as "Red Woven Basket of Flowers."[31]

One professional quiltmaker, Sylvia Pickell, kept a meticulous log of her time making "Immigrant Influences: Album of Heritage."[32] She spent 896 hours on handwork plus 200 hours on design, research, and drawing. Thus 1,096 hours went into making a quilt 72" square, a bit less than half the square footage of the Baltimore Museum of Art's classic Baltimore Bride Quilt (104" square) inscribed "To Miss Elizabeth Sliver" and attributed in the Baltimore Museum catalog to Mary Evans. Sylvia Pickell's reckoning indicates a professional seamstress would need at least a year of 40-hour weeks to make one classic Baltimore Album Quilt about 104" square. Yet the equivalent of well over a dozen quilts have been popularly attributed to one woman, Mary Evans, in roughly a six-year period (1846-1852).

Not only is there an impossible number of quilts attributed to Mary Evans, but additionally, we have only the design style and a method of block preparation to connect to her name. We have no idea how Mary Evans appliquéd: the type, tension, or fineness of her stitch, the color of her thread, or the width and smoothness of her seam. Even when we see identifiable design characteristics, such as the same fabric, or the same skillful draftsmanship, does it prove that one woman made a given block or quilt? I believe not. For one thing, there are significant needlework style differences among blocks attributed to Mary Evans.[33]

To set forth the pivotal differences in style and needlework among the three "Mary Evans" quilts offered for sale January 1989 would require an entire chapter. In short, the quilting of the Sotheby quilt has fewer stitches per inch than the Gorsuch quilt, and both quilts have at least one discolored block suggesting a different foundation fabric or a different age than the surrounding blocks. All three quilts have certain motifs in common. Cornucopias, for example, are found in each, but the blocks differ significantly from quilt to quilt in those elements of style that might separate one maker from another. These elements include fabric use and ink embellishments, how much of the block is filled and in what shape, how compact the bouquets are, and how much white space shows. How are we to know if Mary Evans made some or all of the blocks in any one of these three quilts? What might prove it? Here too, we have the example of contemporary quiltmakers. The current work in classic Baltimore Album style pictured in *Baltimore Beauties and Beyond, Volume I*,[34] shows just how successfully we can both copy and do original designing in this style almost a century and a half later. If quiltmaking today can so successfully imitate vintage Baltimore, then surely copying, changing, and working "in the style of" may have been going on in mid-nineteenth-century Maryland as well.

Attribution to Mary Evans on the popular level has been incautious. Carefully couched opinions and old theories have given way to confident and detailed assertions. The important point is that if quilts aspire to art, then we need also to strive for the standards of authentication required in fine arts. Increasingly, cautious scholars, for example, are careful not to call a quilt a Baltimore Album Quilt unless "Baltimore" is inscribed on it or unless its provenance from that city or county is documentable. If these proofs are lacking in a quilt that seems in all other respects to fill the bill, they call it a "Baltimore-style Album Quilt." We need this kind of responsible standard in both scholarship and in the marketplace. At least four equally ornate and complex Baltimore Album Quilts are supposed to have been made by Evans in the period from 1849-1850: the Metropolitan's Baltimore Album Quilt, recorded in Katzenberg's *Baltimore Album Quilts* as circa 1849 (Photo 26 in *Volume I*); the Baltimore Museum of Art's Album Quilt inscribed "To Miss Elizabeth Sliver" and "Baltimore, 1849" (in this volume's Photo 4-24); the Baltimore Album Quilt inscribed to Dr. John P. Mackenzie and dated "February, 1850"[35]; and Christie's Updegraf family quilt, dated 1850 (quilt #8 in the Color Section). The first three attributions are by Dena Katzenberg, the last, by Christie's. Could Mary Evans, or any one person have made these four quilts in so little time?

The most eloquent, though inconclusive, effort to fix Mary Evan's authorship to specific quilts is Katzenberg's *Baltimore Album Quilts*. The most potentially concrete evidence proposed is that "One signature of a Mary Evans Ford has been discovered on a 1909 application for admittance to the Aged Women's Home. Analysis of that handwriting suggests that it could have belonged to the person credited with almost half of the finest inscriptions on the quilts."[36] I conferred with the personnel in the Documents Laboratory of the Federal Bureau of Investigation[37] to find out if it was possible to ascertain if the signatures, written some sixty years apart, could have been done by the same hand. "Who knows?" one handwriting expert summed up. "You're never going to get a positive identification. I don't know anyone who would even give a leaning under these circumstances."[38]

To sum up, the "dog that didn't bark," convinced me that the Mary Evans attribution in its present form was questionable. Dunton, of all people, was closest to Evans Bramble's attribution of the basted City Springs block to his Great-aunt Mary. Whatever conversation passed between Dr. Dunton and Mr. Bramble, Dunton found that set of blocks "entertaining" but seemingly nothing more. The fact that the "dog didn't bark" when it should have for Dr. Dunton, served for me, as in Arthur Conan Doyle's detective story, as pivotal evidence.

The fact may remain, however, that theories about who made these quilts "cannot be proven" as Dr. Dunton wrote almost a half-century ago. New research efforts, inspired by the reappearance of the City Springs Block (Photo 6-1) and already spearheaded by the Maryland Historical Society, will surely turn up exciting new evidence about who made these quilts and why. But no matter who made the classic Baltimore Album Quilts, they are nonetheless national treasures. These heirlooms bind us to our past, give us continuity in the present, and offer us hope for the future. We may not ever be able to affix specific names with certainty to these quilts' design and manufacture. We can learn more about them, though, and in the process learn more about our culture and our past. By so doing we can help attain for these quilts, the work of so many earnest hands, their due regard.

---

[1] Material in this chapter was presented by the author as a paper titled "The Marketing of Mary Evans" at the American Quilt Study Group annual meeting in Bethesda, Maryland, in October 1989. An extract from that paper was subsequently published in the January 1990 issue of *The Magazine Antiques*, pp. 156, 178, and 206.

[2] Dunton's correspondence in the *Notebooks* includes letters from Florence Peto, who also went into print (*Historic Quilts*, New York, American Historical Co., 1939, p. 103) the year after Dunton recorded the 1938 Springs block/Mary Evans information. Peto echoed Dunton's quest for the professional — but with no mention of Mary Evans: "A feeling persists that many quilts of the Baltimore Bride's type were not made by those whose names were borne on the blocks...."

[3] Rita Reif, "Auctions," *New York Times*, January 13, 1989.

[4] Pat Ferrero, Elaine Hedges, and Julie Silber, *Hearts and Hands: The Influence of Women & Quilts on American Society*, San Francisco, Quilt Digest Press, 1987, p. 36.

[5] "The Market," *Art and Antiques Magazine*, January 1989, p. 46.

[6] *Sotheby's Catalog*, Sale #5680, Lot #1463 (quilt #9 in the Color Section).

[7] *National Antiques Review*, February 1972, p. 21.

[8] Three major antiques sales were held the same January 1989 weekend at Christie's Auction House, Sotheby's Auction House, and the annual New York Winter Antiques Show at the New York Armory.

[9] *Sotheby's Catalog*, Sale #5810, Lot #1106.

[10] Patsy and Myron Orlofsky, *Quilts in America*.

[11] Marilyn Bordes, *Twelve Great Quilts from the American Wing*, New York, Metropolitan Museum of Art, 1974.

[12] Dunton, *Notebooks*, Album VIII, pp.128-35. The text of the seven-page manuscript, dated 1938, reads in part:

Back around 1850 there seems to have been a fashion of making quilts of an unusual character for presentation to some favored man or woman, often a clergyman. It was natural for the ladies of the congregation to show their regard by making a quilt to commemorate his incumbency.

Among the quilts which I have met which are associated with churches or are of this presentation type perhaps the most entertaining is not a quilt but merely the makings as the various blocks have not been joined. One of these was made by Mary Evans Ford (1830-1928) when she was twenty years old, or in 1850, a member of the Caroline Street Methodist Church, not far from City Springs Square, Pratt and Eden Streets, Baltimore, Maryland....

Miss Ford evidently had an attachment to the neighborhood for what was evidently intended to be the large central block of the quilt has in its centre a view of the park with the pavilion which covered the spring or "fountain," done in shaded browns which gives a high light effect to the supporting pillars and also to the trunks of the trees which flank it....The maker was an artist with a wonderful flair for color harmony and of the value of light and shadow so that her perspective is exceptionally well handled. The piece is unfinished as all pieces to be appliquéd are basted on the white ground but the effect is quite beautiful. The muslin is 72 threads to the inch.

Accompanying this which was to have been the centre of an album quilt were six eighteen-inch blocks some of which are signed....The most striking is that depicting the minister which is unsigned....His head and face are partly inked and partly painted. The collar of his coat is broad and is appliquéd separately. His right arm extends down and the painted hand is holding a red edged open book marked "Hymns." His left hand (painted) rests on a tan and yellow book marked "Bible" which is on a red table. Above his head is an inked eagle with a scroll on which is "John W. Hall." (Quoted by permission of Baltimore Museum of Art.)

Dunton then goes on to describe the remaining blocks in the set: One with "quite a conglomeration of symbols" (some that he describes are shared by both Odd Fellows and Masons) and the name, "Nathaniel Lee" inscribed thereon; a "horn" (cornucopia) of "rather ungraceful" flowers and leaves, a heart of "angular leaves" outlined inside and out with a row of quarter-inch berries, and a cutwork square with a "a coarse red rose" on each side and parallel strips of small hexagons intertwined by rosevine. He concludes with subsequent history concerning the City Springs Square and its neighborhood in Baltimore.

[13] Dunton himself long investigated questions raised by the set of seven blocks, as he did so many subjects touched upon by these quilts. His 1938 description of the seven blocks reflects research into the demographics of the City Springs area and the evolution of the Baltimore water system. Two years later, a 1940 letter (in the *Notebook* files) shows that Dunton was still researching the identity of John W. Hall whose name and whose portrait, apparently, appear in one these seven blocks. Page 7 of this Album VIII article gives us yet another clue about John Hall: "It is known that he assisted at laying the cornerstone of Grace Church." This may be a clue to understanding this block, for early histories of Baltimore repeatedly note the laying of various cornerstones in the first half of the nineteenth century as "presided over by the Masons" and as attended by "Masonic ritual."

[14] Dunton, *Old Quilts*, p. 41.

[15] *Ibid.*, p. 118.

[16] Orlofsky, *Quilts in America*, p. 239.

[17] Dena Katzenberg, *Baltimore Album Quilts*, pp. 61-62.

[18] *Ibid.*, p. 98.

[19] Schnuppe Von Gwinner, *The History of the Patchwork Quilt, Origins, Traditions and Symbols of a Textile Art*, Munich, Keyser Book Publishing, 1987, p. 138.

[20] Katzenberg, *Baltimore Album Quilts*, pp. 64-65.

[21] Dunton, *Old Quilts*, pp. 202-203.

[22] *Ibid.*, pp. 195-199.

[23] Ferrero, Hedges, and Silber, *Hearts and Hands*, pp. 34-36.

[24] Katzenberg, *Baltimore Album Quilts*, pp. 61-62.

[25] Frank Donegan, "In the Marketplace: Quiet Time for Quilts," *Americana Magazine*, Fall, 1988, p. 64.

[26] *Quilt Engagement Calendar 1989*; this quilt illustrated May 7-13.

[27] America Hurrah Antiques advertisement, Winter Antiques Show Catalog, January 1989, p. 45, in *The Magazine Antiques*, January 1989, unnumbered advertising page; and in *The Clarion*, Winter 1989, p. 7.

[28] Reif, "Auctions," *New York Times*, January 3, 1989.

[29] This replica was made by the East Bay Heritage Quilters. The estimated hours to quilt this were provided by Adele Ingraham and Janet Shore, leaders of the project.

[30] Sienkiewicz, *Baltimore Beauties and Beyond, Volume I*, Color Plate 24.

[31] *Ibid.*, Color Plate 35.

[32] *Ibid.*, Photo 31.

[33] *Ibid.* pp.102-103.

[34] *Ibid.*, pp. 81-96 and 107.

[35] Dunton, *Old Quilts*, pp. 31-43; and Roxa Wright, "Baltimore Friendship Quilt," *Woman's Day Magazine*, Fall 1965, pp. 52, 53, and 90.

[36] Katzenberg, *Baltimore Album Quilts*, p. 62. Further discussion of signatures is found on pp. 68-69.

[37] Bill Carter of the Federal Bureau of Investigation Press Department, co-ordinator, with FBI Documents Laboratory personnel, interview by the author, Washington, D.C., February 28, 1989.

[38] Another expert added, "Even your own handwriting changes over the years. Injury, illness, even the intention to change your own handwriting affects it. When we do handwriting comparisons we don't like to deal with writing that is over five years apart [from the identified specimen]. You cannot associate writing without same-time writing samples."

"Could you ever say positively that one person could have written many different names on these quilts?" I asked. The response was, "Absolutely not. There might be some letter combinations in common that might suggest a possibility, however remote. But the phrases being compared [or the names being signed] have to be the same for purposes of positively identifying authorship." Katzenberg offers both diverse names and varied inscriptions for comparison to Mary Evans Ford's signature (pp. 62 and 68 in *Baltimore Album Quilts*). Furthermore, it was noted in the interview that the samples would have to be "natural and free-flowing and on the same surface," not a comparison between one done on paper and others done on fabric. "Writing with ink on fabric is by definition contrived, not natural and free-flowing."

Observing that greater uniformity of penmanship and closer conformity to a calligraphic ideal were characteristic of the mid-nineteenth century, one expert said, "They were stricter then. The longer a person stayed with an intent to write in the Copperplate Hand, the chances are even less that an association could be made." She noted that she could not connect my signature on a free-flowing letter with my careful signature on a quilt block.

Part Two: The Quiltmakers

Gratitude

JoAnne Parisi

About the Needleartists Whose Work Appears in Baltimore Beauties and Beyond, Volume II

A contest was held in 1984 asking entrants to reproduce, or base a block on, a design from the author's first book, *Spoken Without a Word*. There were ten winners. These contest winners were the inspiration for this *Baltimore Beauties* series and their names are listed in full in *Volume I*. These latter-day good "Ladies of Baltimore" were later joined by other needleartists, including master quilters. Additional artists appear with their work in the pattern companion to *Volume I* (*Baltimore Album Quilts — Historic Notes and Antique Patterns*), the pattern companion to *Volume II*, and *Volume III*. These ladies' enthusiasm and generosity have been essential to both the quilts which they helped make, and to *Baltimore Beauties and Beyond*. These women, every one, have my profound gratitude. The brief remarks here are based on replies to the author's needleartist questionnaires. Note: Biographical notes on needleartists tend to appear only once in the series even though their work may appear in several volumes.

LAURA B. ANTHONY, *Washington, D.C.: Variation on the Numsen Family Lyre Wreath.*

"My grandmother quilted. When I quilt, I feel a link with her and a whole chain of women I don't know and their everyday life experiences. Quilting slows me down if I go too fast — it's calming. I take it with me everywhere. It keeps me patient. A piece of it is my pleasure in seeing pattern and shape and light." Laura is mother to three and also serves as the Educational Specialist for the Ward III representative on the D.C. school board. With an art major from Wellesley College, she has designed a quilt for her daughter and also the 1990 Ben W. Murch Elementary School Auction Quilt. She is part of the Murch Friendship Quilters as well.

DONNA COLLINS, *Bridgeport, New York: Goose Girl, Tropical Boating, "Petite Baltimore Album"* (quilt #16).

Donna's prolific creation of quilts is matched only by the fineness of her stitches. The masterpiece of her miniatures is "Petite Baltimore Album," based on six-inch-block versions of the patterns given in *Spoken Without a Word*. The fabric in that quilt is all hand-dyed by New York Beauty Fabric and Design. Donna teaches quiltmaking and sells her miniatures and patterns.

MONA CUMBERLEDGE, *Alma, West Virginia: Quilting of "Odense Album."*

A native West Virginian, Mona started quilting at 12 or 13, joining in at neighborhood quilting bees. Mother of two daughters and grandmother to four, Mona works for the state's Division of Human Services. Living on a small farm which is "more like a hobby," Mona keeps a quilt in all the time, saying "my frames haven't been empty for several years now."

ELLIE DAWSON, *Camp Springs, Maryland: Rosebud Wreathed Heart.*

Trained in commercial art, and both Western traditional and sumi-e painting, Ellie took up quiltmaking in 1988. Taught first to sew as a child by her grandmother, Ellie is now a member of the Annapolis Quilt Guild.

EAST BAY HERITAGE QUILTERS, *San Francisco Bay Area, California: "Baltimore Album Redone." Group quilt started October 1986 and finished June 1988. Pattern drafted by Adele Ingraham from the Metropolitan Museum of Art's poster of their classic Baltimore-style Album Quilt. Fabric selected by Adele and by Janet Shore. Thirty members of EBHQ appliquéd the top, and more than six members quilted it.*

This spectacular quilt was to be the guild's 1988 raffle quilt, but they couldn't bear to part with it. Three members machine-made a second, more modern, quilt for the raffle. Fortuitously, the generous winner donated the second quilt back to the guild that the two quilts should stay together with the East Bay Heritage Quilters. Author's note: While observing "Baltimore Album Redone" closely at a 1989 Exhibit at Sauder Village in Ohio, I heard a voice from a small cluster of Mennonite quiltmakers: "There, you can see that this quilting was all done by one woman. All the stitches are so fine and even." To which there was nodded agreement.

SALLY J. GLAZE, *Austin, Texas: Goose Girl Milking (in Heart Medallion Frame).*

"Originally from St. Louis, we are now living in Austin, Texas, to be near our children and grandchildren, I've found a world of quilt lovers and quiltmakers. My plan is now to develop my love for appliqué and traditional quilts."

JULIE HART, *West Des Moines, Iowa: Squared Grapevine Wreath.*

A CPA with an MBA, Julie has been a quilter for just two years, and writes, "Quilting is so versatile, from 'create and produce' moods at the sewing machine to treasured quiet moments alone with appliqué when I absent myself briefly from my home, my wonderful husband, and my two busy little boys. The shared fellowship with other quiltmakers, in part, makes this art so enjoyable."

RENA M. HEFLEY, *Charleston, South Carolina: Gone With the Wind (Photo 3-3).*

"I love to quilt and am always willing to try something new. Perfecting my appliqué and learning Japanese *sashiko* quilting are next on my list. I love to make gifts for my family and friends, so I have very little at home of my own work." Of her blocks, she writes, "The figures were adapted from my pattern for the 'Little Women Quilt.'"

KAY HUNZINGER, *Phoenix, Arizona: Hans Christian Andersen's Danish Hearts.*

Kay was brought up in rural Mississippi with a love for handmade things. Despite a full-time job and family, she manages "to do something quilt-related" every day. "With my two sons now married, there is more time to devote to my Baltimore Album Quilt." During the time Kay was working on this block, her mother-in-law Lena Rose Hunzinger died. In remembrance, her name is inscribed on Kay's block.

MARGARET FLEISCHER KAUFMAN, *Kentfield, California: Poems: "Old Quilts" and "Deep in the Territory."*

"I am a poet and writer of short fiction, stitching wonder instead of cloth. I collect quilts — they connect me to other women's lives — and I live in California with my husband and three children."

JEAN WELLS KEENAN, *Sisters, Oregon: Duty, Honor, Country (Photo 3-4).*

"I've been sewing all my life and have made quilting a career. I own the Stitchin' Post, and have written numerous quilt books. I'm very fortunate to be able to make a living at what I love doing." Jean's books include *Fans, A Celebration of Hearts*, and her latest, *Picture This* (all from C & T Publishing).

KATHLEEN REILLY MANNIX, *Washington, D.C.: Hearts and Hand in a Feather Wreath.*

Kathy attributes her good eye for color to her family. "I am a Washington native and my parents took me to museums and fine arts shows regularly. My grandmother, Daisy Wightman, taught me to match colors and piece at nine. I learned to do the actual quilting in a class taught by my neighbor, Elly Sienkiewicz. That was a dozen years ago when both our daughters were young." Kathy majored in elementary education at George Washington University, and has contributed her "good eye" and more to the preparation of *Baltimore Album Quilts — Historic Notes and Antique Patterns* and *Volume II.*

RUTH H. MEYERS, *Dhahran, Saudi Arabia: Bird in a Fruit Wreath.*

"An article by the Gutcheons started me quilting in Saudi Arabia where we have lived since 1975. I like to do contemporary interpretations of quilts using my own dyed and printed fabrics. My taste is more abstract than realistic and I like trying to capture a mood in natural subjects. I've done commission work including a series of "Garden Quilts" based on Paradise in the Koran and a full Baltimore Album Quilt in classic style. Once a year, my new work is exhibited with the Dhahran Art Group.

JO ANNE PARISI, *West Springfield, Massachusetts: Rosebud Wreathed Heart.*

Crochet first caught Jo Anne's fancy when she was just 12. Other needlework forms appealed until she began quilting a dozen years ago. Since then she has been happily engrossed in the quilt world, from running a shop in her home, to opening the Calico Stitchery Quilt Shop, to teaching quiltmaking.

SUSAN RUNGE, *Mt. Pleasant, South Carolina: Quilting design, quilting, and binding of "More Maryland Flowers," quilt #13.*

"About ten years ago I decided to pursue the opportunity to express my preferences, personality, and creativity through fabric. Now I enjoy surrounding myself with dear quilting friends and the Cobblestone Quilters' Guild. Working full-time as business manager in the Department of Anatomy at the Medical University is rewarding, but takes a bite out of my quilting time!"

LISA DEBEE SCHILLER, *Houston, Texas: Wreath of Hearts I and II.*

Educated as an interior designer, Lisa spent eight years drafting for engineering and architectural firms before taking up quiltmaking six years ago. Lisa appliquéd panels on the American International Quilting Association's quilt displayed in Salzburg, Austria, in 1989. The classes she teaches on Baltimore-style quiltmaking at "Great Expectations" quilt shop in Houston, Texas, reflect the warmth, enthusiasm, industry, and talent that Lisa pours into them.

JUDY SEVERSON, *San Rafael, California: Elly's Heart (Photo 5-2).*

Judy is a printmaker specializing in embossed quilt prints; in the evenings, she quilts for her own enjoyment. Fascinated by quilt history, she enjoys studying traditional quilts. Stuffed work and background quilting are as important to her as the quilt patterns. She is happy that her quiltmaking and printmaking go hand in hand.

ELEANOR PATTON HAMILTON SIENKIEWICZ, *Washington, D.C.: Crossed Pine Cones and Rosebuds, Numsen Family Lyre, Star with Fleur-de-Lis and Rosebuds, Heart Medallion Frame with Katya and Her Cats, Acorn and Oak Leaf Frame (The Sienkiewiczes at Home). Design only of border corners to Patterns #21 and #22, Hans Christian Andersen's Danish Hearts, Goose Girl Milking in Heart Medallion Frame, Fleur-de-Lis and Rosebuds IV, and border and inkwork for quilt #17.*

Since writing and self-publishing her first book on Baltimore Album Quilts, *Spoken Without a Word* in 1983, Elly's fascination with these particular quilts seems only to have deepened. Her interest is as much in the history and culture reflected by these quilts as in the unparalleled beauty of their design. She finds the simpler blocks, the inking of them, and the sleuthing for the symbolic meaning in these quilts the most personally compelling.

SHIZUE TSURUMOTO, *Meitoku, Nagoya, Japan: Quilt #15.*

Ms. Tsurumoto is a professional quiltmaker and teacher in Japan. She has made numerous appliqué quilts and her work has been published and exhibited widely. She has a beautiful color sense and a love for working in antique kimono silks. Her study of the Baltimore quilts has brought her to take classes in the United States.

AUDREY WAITE, *Sedona, Arizona: Fleur-de-Lis with Rosebuds III (Photo pattern given in Baltimore Album Quilts — Historic Notes and Antique Patterns), piecing of sashing and setting together of "Odense Album," quilt #17.*

Audrey started collecting antique quilts in 1976 and began quilting in 1977. Appreciating nineteenth-century quilts, especially those of Baltimore, Audrey decided to surprise her husband on their twenty-fifth wedding anniversary with one from her own hand. A year of stolen moments later was insufficient time, so he was surprised, all right — with a box of a few completed blocks and lots of

pieces! Nonetheless, her husband fondly calls her the "quilt top queen," as working part-time and serving on the Arizona Quilt Project board leaves little time to complete these projected quilts.

SUSAN ALICE YANUZ, *Rockford, Michigan: Appliqué of the entire border of "More Maryland Flowers," quilt #13.*

"My Gramma Klastow started teaching me to sew when I was seven. I started with flannel shirts for my brothers, then stamped cross-stitch and embroidery. I've loved sewing and especially handstitching ever since." Susan appliquéd the quilt's peony border with great efficiency, and adds "I loved the freezer-paper-on-the-top method!"

QUILT #13. *"More Maryland Flowers," Group Quilt, 1984-1990. Design (of quilt and border), setting together, inkwork, and blocks A-1, A-4, B-2, and C-3 by Elly Sienkiewicz. Appliqué of border by Susan Yanuz. Quilting custom designed and sewn by Susan Runge. Blocks made by Eloise Lewis McCartney (design and fabrication of A-2), Daphne Hedges (B-1), Joy Nichols (design and fabrication of B-3 and C-2), and Agnes M. Cook (C-1). Patterns for blocks B-1 and C-1 are in* Spoken Without a Word.)

This is the last and smallest of three quilts originating from the 1984 contest. (The first two are quilts #6 and #7 in *Volume I.*) When setting this quilt together in 1987, Elly was thinking ahead to her twentieth wedding anniversary in June of 1989. Following tradition, she made this a presentation quilt, dedicating it by center-block inscription to her husband, Stan Sienkiewicz. Inscriptions on other blocks and even the name, "More Maryland Flowers," refer to Stan's ongoing avocation — building house, terraced gardens, and dock on a small parcel on the Severn River, just twenty minutes from Baltimore.

QUILT #17. *"Odense Album," Group quilt. 1989-1990. Design (of quilt and border) and inkwork, by Elly Sienkiewicz; border fabric arrangement and appliqué by Albertine Veenstra; sashings and set by Audrey Waite; quilted by Mona Cumberledge. Blocks made by Ellie Dawson, Shirley Hedman, Lucy Rogers Matteo, Mary Wise Miller, Jo Anne Parisi, Elly Sienkiewicz (2), Audrey Waite, and Gene Way.*

The prospect of an international quilt convention, Quilt Expo Europa 1990 in Denmark, inspired this special friendship Album Quilt. Asked to teach appliqué at the conference, Elly Sienkiewicz sought to personalize the course to the convention site: Odense. A bit of research revealed that Odense was the birthplace of the beloved writer of fairy tales, Hans Christian Andersen, and further, that he was also an artist. His numerous paper-cuttings were sometimes inscribed, then carefully pasted into those famed Victorian albums as mementos. Cherished still, many have found their way safely back to the Hans Christian Andersen Museum in Odense.

"What a pity America lies so far away," wrote Andersen. But the pull was strong. A picture book, William Cullen Bryant's *Picturesque America*, and two hundred dollars were sent as a gift to Andersen in 1874. The money had been donated by American schoolchildren. It is clear from the way he wrote about America that Andersen would have been so pleased at a later gift, a gift of his statue in bronze, by Otto F. Langmann. Made in 1956, this portrait of Andersen, seated, reading *The Ugly Duckling*, is in Central Park, New York City, a generous contribution to us all from the Danish-American Women's Association. It is pictured in one of the blocks that flank the quilt's center (block A-2), as is the statue, *The Little Mermaid of Copenhagen* (block C-2).

The heart medallions on the border read: #I (bottom): "The Odense Album Quilt made in honor of Hans Christian Andersen, Odense's Victorian Era Native Son, who wrote of his fairy tales, 'My Gift to the world.' Quilt Expo Europa, 1990." #II (side): "Placement of the border's varied fabrics and appliqué and stitchery embellishment of the quilt's running border were done by Albertine Veenstra, of Acton, Massachusetts. That the quilt's completion should run on time, Albertine worked intensely, sewing this border in under six weeks during December and January, 1989-1990." #III (side): "The quilt's sashings were drafted and sewn by Audrey Waite of Mesa, Arizona who also set the quilt together. In less than two months, Mona Cumberledge of Alma, West Virginia quilted and bound this Album that it should be complete in time for Quilt Expo Europa, 1990." #IV (top): "The Odense Album was designed by Elly Sienkiewicz who made two of the blocks and who did the quilt's inkwork. Seven American quiltmakers sewed the blocks and their names and states are inscribed thereon. This quilt hung in the Hans Christian Andersen Museum in Odense during Quilt Expo in May 1990. A commemorative block designed and stitched by Elly Sienkiewicz was presented to the Mayor of Odense at that time."

Part Three: The Patterns

The patterns for twenty blocks are given here on one, two, and four pages. The pattern transfer method for block designs depends on the number of pages as explained in "Part One: Getting Started" in *Volume I*. The thirteen border patterns are given as Edging Motifs or as Central Motifs. They can be used separately or mixed and matched on a given border. When I have had to make up a pattern name, I note this with an asterisk(*). Symbolic meanings for an appliquéd pattern are taken from *Spoken Without a Word* unless otherwise noted.

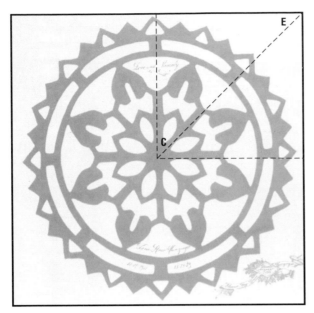

PATTERN #1: "Hans Christian Andersen's Danish Hearts"*

Type: "Beyond" Baltimore
To make this block, refer to *Volume I*, Lesson 1, 2, or 11.

"Godfather could tell stories, cut pictures, and draw," wrote Hans Christian Andersen, seemingly of himself. This circle of hearts is a close facsimile of one of Hans Christian Andersen's nineteenth-century paper-cuts, now exquisitely appliquéd by Eleanor Kay Green Hunzinger of Phoenix, Arizona. Elly Sienkiewicz drafted the pattern (and added the triangle edging) for a course in "Andersen and Appliqué," taught at Quilt Expo Europa in Andersen's birthplace, Odense, Denmark.

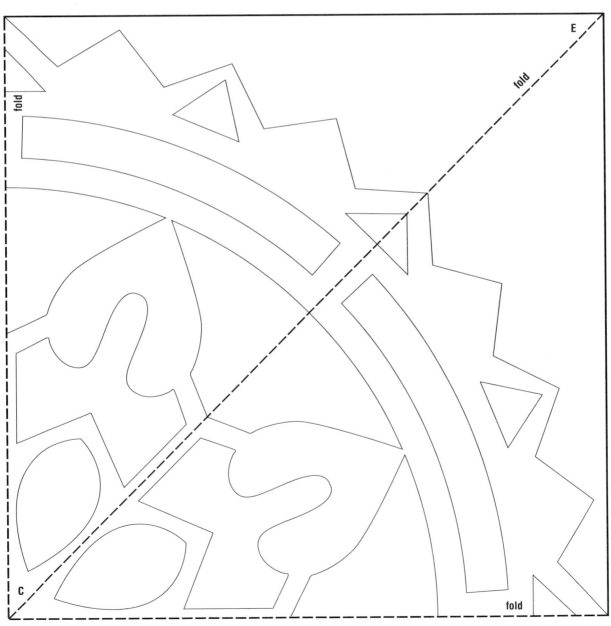

PATTERN #2: "Square Wreath with Fleur-de-Lis and Rosebuds"*

Type: Classic Baltimore from the Album "made by Mrs. Mary Everist, circa 1847-1850" in the collection of the Baltimore Museum of Art
To make this block, refer to *Volume I*, Lesson 1 or 4.

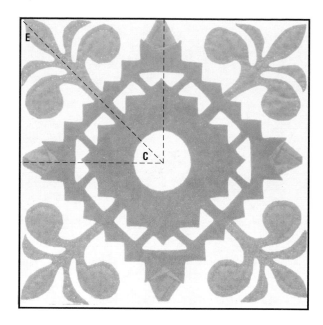

A seemingly unique version of the relentlessly popular "fleur-de-lis, rosebud, and square wreath" block, this one is both dramatic and intriguing. For, were one to read the fleur-de-lis as the national emblem of France, and the rose for Love, one might see this block as a tribute to the Marquis de Lafayette, "the hero of two continents," "the apostle of liberty." How? Lafayette's farewell tour of America in 1824-1825 produced a major artistic outpouring from Americans, Baltimoreans not the least. Lafayette was an ardent Mason, and his wife is said to have made the Masonic apron which George Washington wore to lay the cornerstone of the Nation's Capitol. Bespeaking Masonry, the center of this block reads almost as a "geometry sampler" with the square, the circle, and triangles. And geometry is "the basis on which the superstructure of freemasonry is erected," according to *The True Masonic Chart* (p. 32).

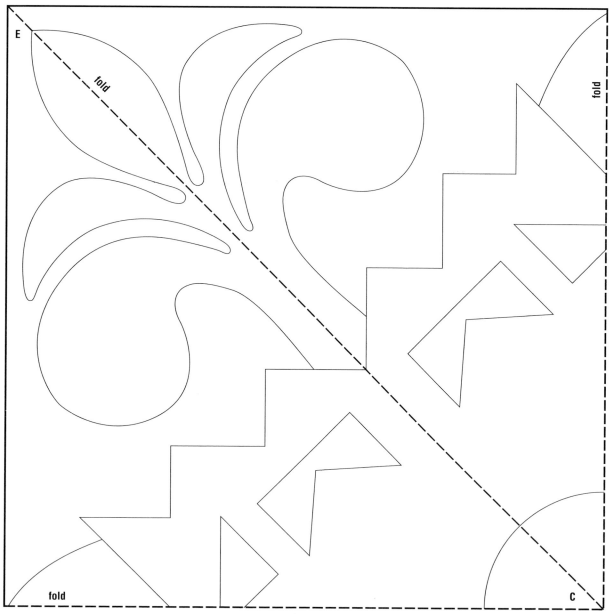

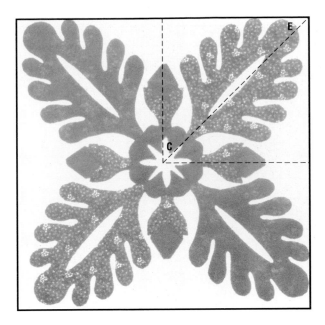

PATTERN #3: "Crossed Pine Cones and Rosebuds"*

Type: Classic Baltimore
To make this block, refer to *Volume I*, Lesson 5.

There are innumerable versions of pine cone blocks. The fact that this object was so oft repeated in the classic Baltimore Album Quilts, yet was sometimes almost homely in rendition was, for me, an early clue to its symbolic intent. Pine cones symbolize Fertility or Fruitfulness because of the pine's many seeds. The pine tree was an important symbol for freedom in Revolutionary times, and the wooden pole often seen in patriotic eagle blocks would be the pine "liberty pole." Using the terms "pine" and "cone" differently, Dr. Dunton in *Old Quilts* (p. 209) writes of their ancient symbolism (Fertility and the Creator) in connection with the date palm.

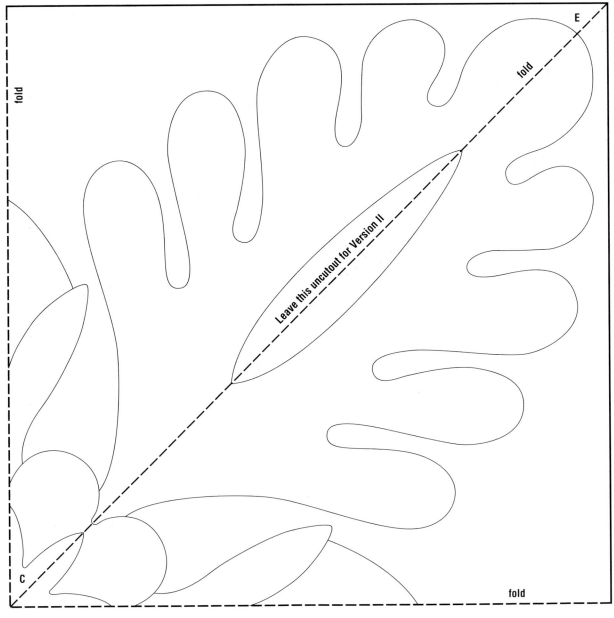

Leave this uncutout for Version II

PATTERN #4: "Joy Nichol's Rose of Sharon"*

Type: "Beyond" Baltimore
To make this block, refer to *Volume I*, Lesson 9 and 10. See also
Baltimore Album Quilts — Historic Notes and Antique Patterns,
Appendix I.

This pattern, which I call the Rose of Sharon but which, according to Cuesta Benberry, may be the President's Wreath, recurs
repeatedly in the classic Baltimore Album Quilts. By either name,
its inclusion would be significant as well as beautiful. Joy's fabric
use in this version of her design is rich, textural in appearance,
and charming.

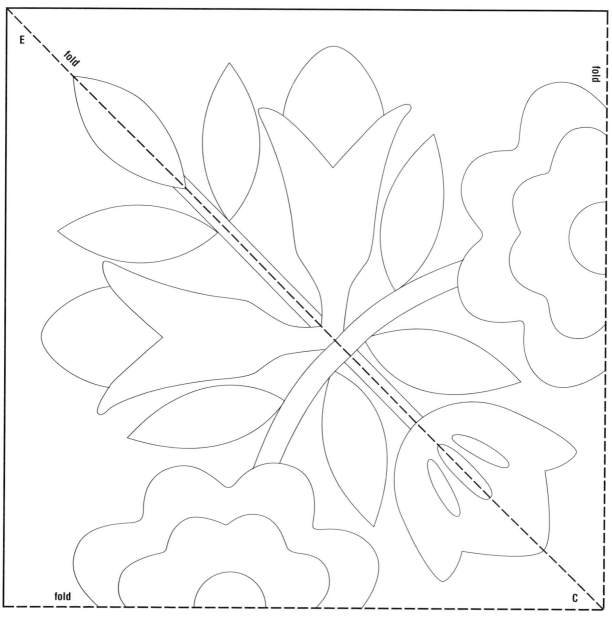

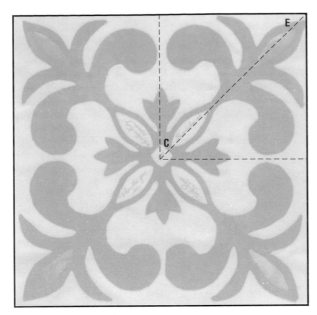

PATTERN #5: "Fleur-de-Lis III"*

Type: "Beyond" Baltimore
To make this block, refer to *Volume I*, Lesson 1, 2, or 11.

This is an elegant yet relatively simple version of the popular fleur-de-lis cut-out. It is a design I made by paper-cutting, here artfully rendered in fabric by Kathy Pease. Made in a large-scale, rich red print, the pattern can be used with other similar blocks to create an interior pattern within your quilt. Traditional interior patterns are square-on-point medallions made of eight blocks, or Greek crosses. Yet a different sort of cross has been formed by predominantly red blocks in *Volume I*'s quilt #6.

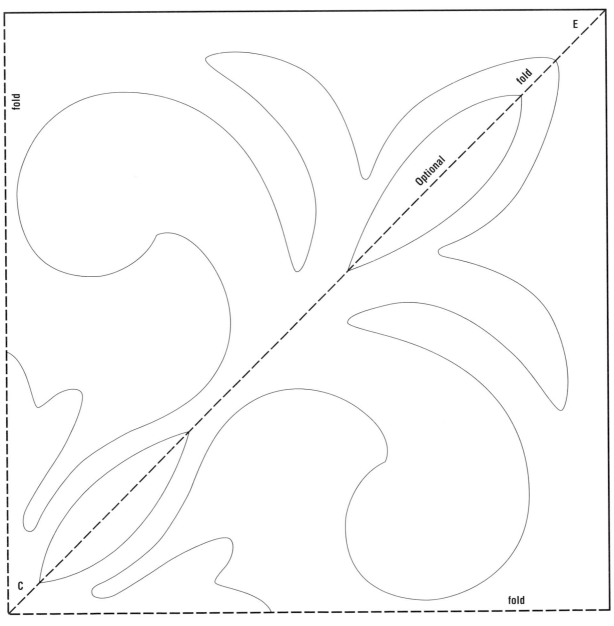

PATTERN #6: "Acorn and Oak Leaf Frame"*

Type: "Beyond" Baltimore
To make this block, refer to *Volume I*, Lesson 1, 2, or 11.

Botanical themes provide an endless source for designing your own picture-block frames. Because the acorn symbolizes Longevity and Immortality, the oak's leaves, Courage, and the oak tree, Strength against Adversity, this seemed the perfect choice of magic with which to wrap this portrait of my husband and me. Any one of the picture-block frames would also make an ideal enclosure for an inscription.

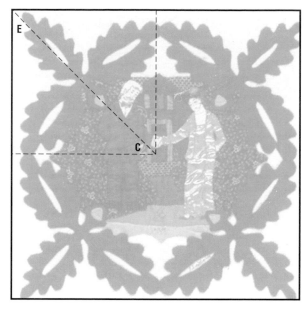

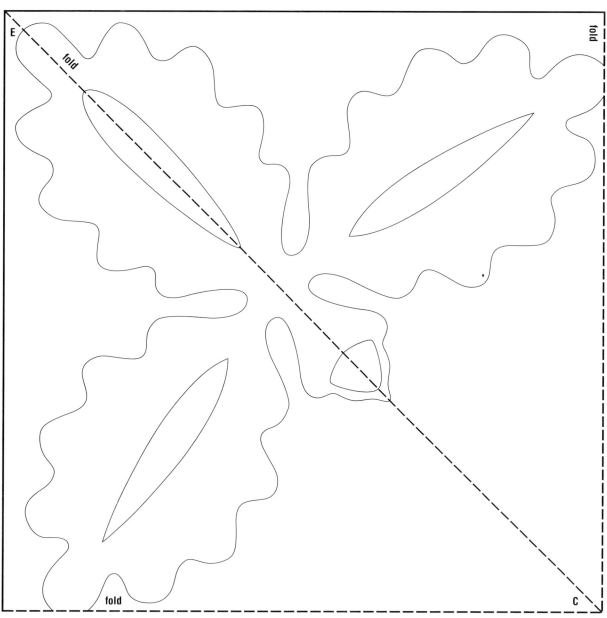

PATTERN #7: "Heart Medallion Frame"*

Type: "Beyond" Baltimore
To make this block, refer to *Volume I*, Lesson 1, 2, or 11.

I designed this and the Acorn and Oak Leaf Frame as picture-block frames which would work well with the classic red *scherenschnitte* frame seen on the Hunting Scene pattern in *Spoken Without a Word* and in its original in quilt #10 in the Color Section. Small yellow candy kiss shapes accent the corners. In the block, Katya and Her Cats, however, I forgot to include them. See *Volume I*, quilt #6, for a color picture of these blocks and to see how several framed blocks can help create an interior design in the quilt's set.

PATTERN #8: "Goose Girl Milking"*

Type: "Beyond" Baltimore
To make this block, refer to *Volume I*, Lesson 5 or 10. See also
Baltimore Album Quilts — Historic Notes and Antique Patterns,
Appendix I.

This scene fits the previous pattern, Heart Medallion Frame, and was inspired by a classic Album scene. One wonders what subject, what thought, encouraged these infrequent yet recurring bucolic scenes of a young lady with furred and feathered friends. Beautifully appliquéd here by Sally Glaze, the Heart Medallion Frame takes on a different look in an overall feathered red print.

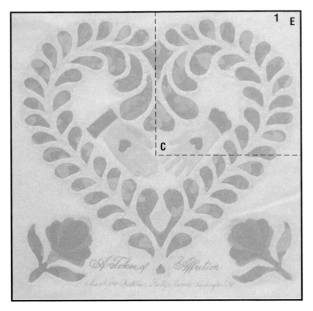

PATTERN #9: "Hearts and Hands in a Feather Wreath"*

Type: "Beyond" Baltimore

To make this block, refer to *Volume I*, Lesson 1, 2, 3, or 10. See also *Baltimore Album Quilts — Historic Notes and Antique Patterns*, Appendix I.

This is a third version of the feather-wreathed hearts which I designed for *Volume I*. It was never made because of the increasing difficulty in finding high-quality off-white background fabric which does not fray too badly for reverse appliqué. Kathy Mannix, my friend and neighbor, suggested that one of the printed white-on-white muslins might work well and proceeded to make this lovely block. She reports that it turned like butter and that the appliqué, petal by petal, is like eating candy — hard to stop!

PATTERN #9: "Hearts and Hands in a Feather Wreath"*

(Second page)

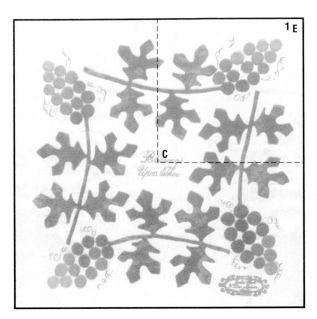

PATTERN #10: "Squared Grapevine Wreath"*

Type: Classic Baltimore from the quilt in the collection of the Baltimore Museum of Art
To make this block, refer to *Volume I*, Lessons 1, 2, and 9.

This block fascinated me. It was such an unusual (infrequent, but repeated) stylization by which to depict grapes. I speculated that it would have made a good teaching block with stems, circles, points — and wondered if the pattern had been taught as an appliqué sample at some ladies' academy of the period, one accessible to Baltimoreans. It seemed almost like mental telepathy, then, when a version of this block caught my eye in the quilt labeled "Oxford Female Seminary Album Quilt, 1846" (Photo 4-6). To complete this pattern, rotate the grape bunch clockwise.

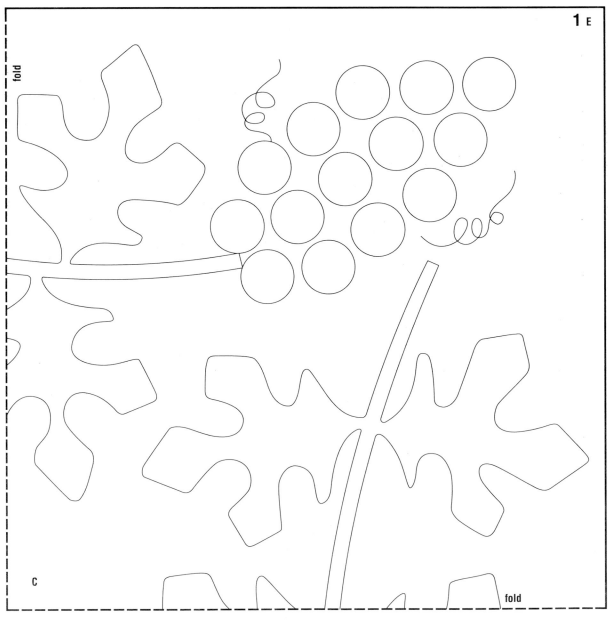

PATTERN #10: "Squared Grapevine Wreath"*

(Second Page)

Blessings
Upon Thee

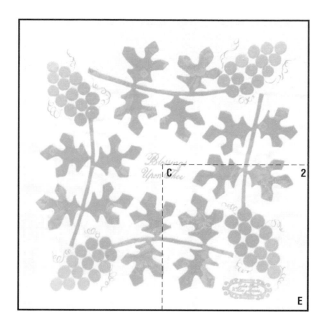

PATTERN #11: "Numsen Family Lyre"*

Type: Classic Baltimore
To make this block, refer to *Volume I*, Lessons 5 and 10. See also *Baltimore Album Quilts — Historic Notes and Antique Patterns*, Appendix I.

I first saw this simple and very sculptural lyre in a floral wreath in the Numsen I quilt, then again in the Numsen II quilt in the same fabrics (see *Volume III*), and again in these fabrics in yet a third quilt recently discovered in the Virginia quilt search but with no name written upon it. In the Numsen II quilt, this block bears the inscription, "Sophia C. Numsen." Based on a Numsen family genealogy, at least four quilts (one being quilt #11 in the Color Section) bear Numsen family names. According to that

PATTERN #11: "Numsen Family Lyre"*

(Second Page)

genealogy, young Sophia — and some friends who married into the family — were of a marrying age when those quilts were made. Perhaps this graphic and relatively quick block was the one Sophia repeated to give the others for their Albums? I have thought that if I needed such a quick and easy block for giving, the Ruched Rose Lyre block from *Volume I* would be my favorite. By using cutwork appliqué for all the green, and red soutache for the lyre strings, this Numsen Family Lyre was equally appealing to make.

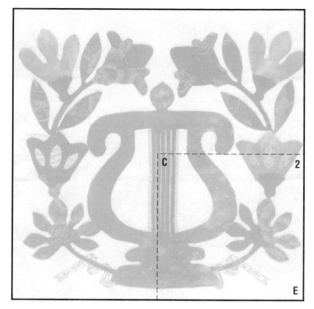

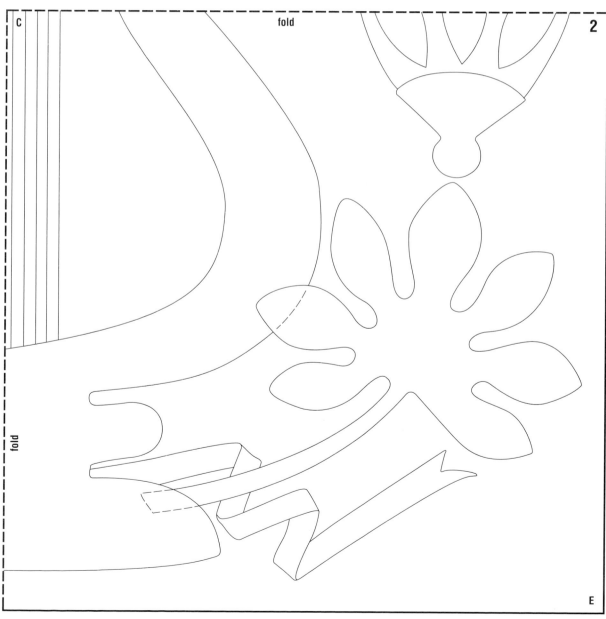

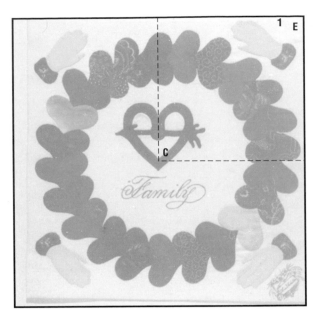

PATTERN #12: "Wreath of Hearts I"* (and II)

Type: Wreath of Hearts I is classic Baltimore and appears as a simple circle of hearts in the circa 1850 Album Quilt pictured in the *Quilt Engagement Calendar Treasury* (p. 148)
To make this block, refer to *Volume I*, Lesson 10.

While Version II is "beyond" Baltimore, being of my own design, it looks quite Victorian and Baltimorean in Lisa Schiller's fine appliqué and fabrics. In part this vintage look comes from the heart, the hand, and the arrow — all Odd Fellow symbols which recur in the vintage Albums. Fraternal orders used symbols to teach precepts. Thus the arrow teaches the Odd Fellow "to make all efforts to save a brother when he is in peril; ... the heart and hand urge the Odd Fellow to acts of mercy and benevolence; and it is intended also to refer to the spirit in which those acts are to be performed" (*Odd Fellows Monitor and Guide*, p. 47). And do these not seem appropriate symbols for family precepts as well?

PATTERN #12: "Wreath of Hearts I"* (and II)

(Second page)

Family

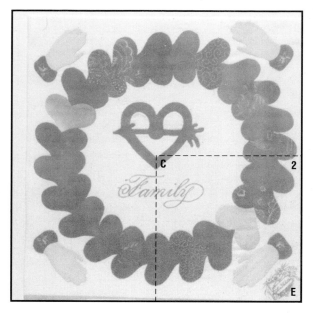

C

fold   2

Heart Template

fold

E

PATTERN #13: "Bird in a Fruit Wreath"*

Type: Classic Baltimore (from quilt #4 in *Baltimore Album Quilts — Historic Notes and Antique Patterns*)
To make this block, refer to *Volume I*, Lesson 10. See also *Baltimore Album Quilts — Historic Notes and Antique Patterns*, Appendix I.

Take up birdwatching in the classic Baltimore Albums and you will be richly rewarded. Though made in a temperate clime, those "natural history albums" are filled with tropical birds, exotic newly met species brought back under sail or steam from Africa and South America to be engraved in illustrated folios. There are, in these quilts, toucans, small African parrots ("love birds"), peacocks, and birds better known in that Audubon/Album Quilt era than now. But there are also doves, hummingbirds, thistle-finches ("distlefinks"), and eagles. I am quite sure that in the original block this was meant to be some very specific real bird, perhaps a sparrow, here beautifully wrought anew by Ruth Meyers.

PATTERN #13: "Bird in a Fruit Wreath"*

(Second page)

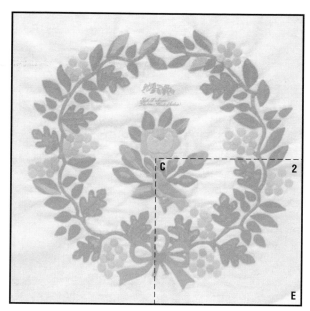

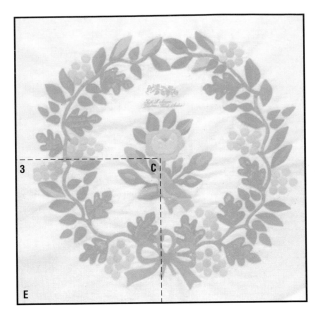

PATTERN #13: "Bird in a Fruit Wreath"*

(Third page)

PATTERN #13: "Bird in a Fruit Wreath"*

(Fourth page)

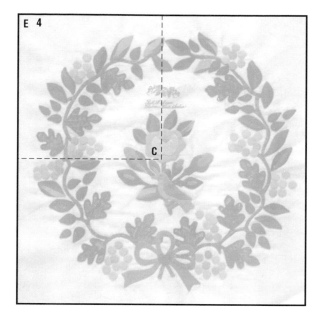

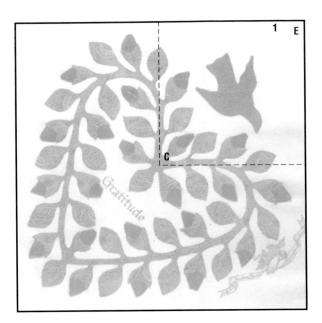

PATTERN #14: "Rosebud Wreathed Heart"*

Type: "Beyond" Baltimore
To make this block, refer to *Volume I*, Lessons 1 or 2, 5 and 6.

This pattern is based on an upright rosebud-wreathed heart, block C-1 in the Baltimore Album Quilt, 1847-1848, made for Reverend Dr. George C. M. Roberts, and now in the collection of Lovely Lane Museum, Baltimore (see Photo 4-15). I designed this version as a diagonal block that would guide the eye inward from the outside corners of a quilt. Two models for this block were made by Ellie Dawson and Jo Anne Parisi in the "Odense Album," quilt #17 in the Color Section. To unify that quilt, the bird from Cherry-Wreathed Heart in *Baltimore Album Quilts — Historic Notes and Antique Patterns* was substituted for the dove in this pattern.

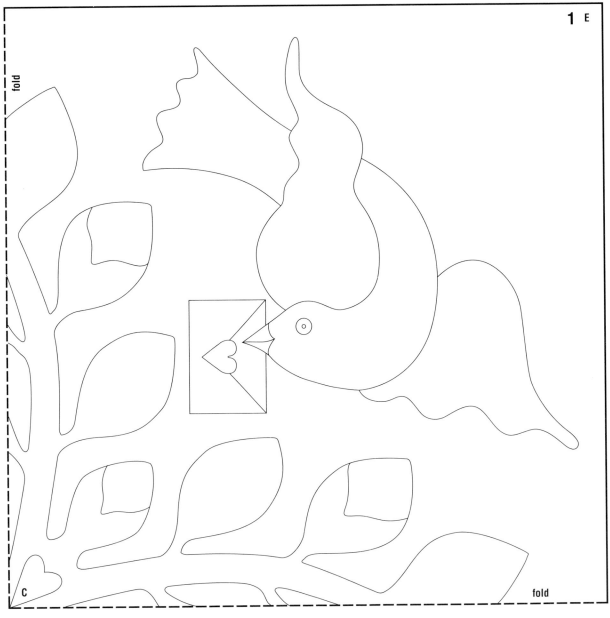

PATTERN #14: "Rosebud Wreathed Heart"*

(Second page)

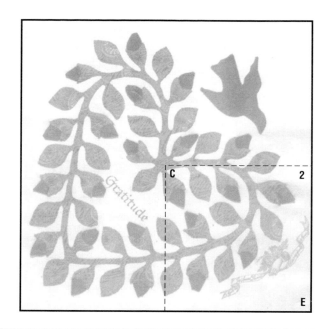

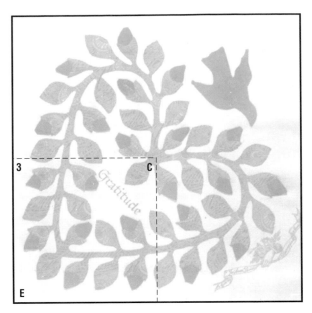

PATTERN #14: "Rosebud Wreathed Heart"*

(Third page)

PATTERN #14: "Rosebud Wreathed Heart"*

(Fourth page)

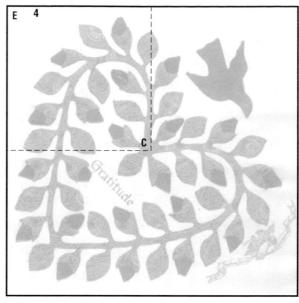

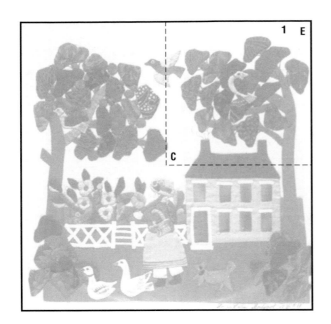

PATTERN #15: "Goose Girl"*

Type: Baltimore-style

To make this block, refer to *Volume I*, Lesson 10. See also *Baltimore Album Quilts — Historic Notes and Antique Patterns*, Appendix I.

As a classic quilt block, this scene comes in several versions. One wonders what the important elements in it are and whether it has some symbolic significance. For example, one Numsen family house/garden scene, which we will discuss in *Volume III*, shows the house, the fence, the trees, the birds, but instead of the girl walking, there is an empty path with an ornate and bustling silk beehive at its end. And might the Georgian House pictured in Photo 4-13 (block C-5) be intended to convey something of the same subject matter with its ten birds and two-and-a-half circles on the lawn? Beyond such mysteries, Donna Collin's version here seems even more beautiful than any of its classic predecessors.

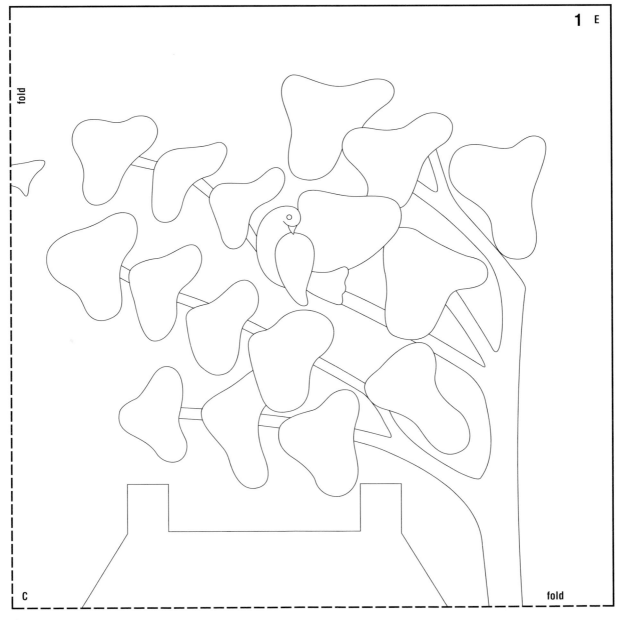

PATTERN #15: "Goose Girl"*

(Second page)

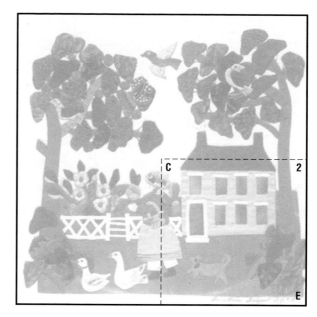

PATTERN #15: "Goose Girl"*

(Third page)

PATTERN #15: "Goose Girl"*

(Fourth page)

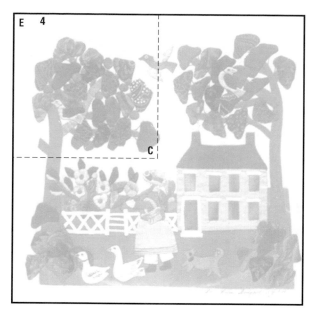

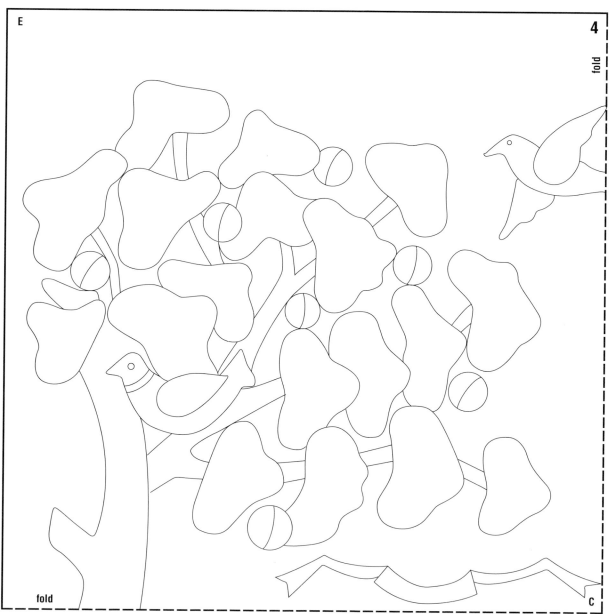

PATTERN #16: "Waterfowling"*

Type: Baltimore-style

To make this block, refer to *Volume I*, Lesson 5 or 10. See also *Baltimore Album Quilts — Historic Notes and Antique Patterns*, Appendix I.

Though relatively rare, picture blocks of men waterfowling are repeated in the classic quilts. A detail of quilt #10 (block C-4) illustrates the layout of our pattern, but the pattern itself offers yet another classic interpretation of the theme. Quilt #10's square includes someone boating while the pattern taken from another quilt has a boat at anchor. The human characters vary in these hunting scenes, but fowl are always plentiful and a bird dog or two is always along. Dogs symbolize Fidelity and occur elsewhere

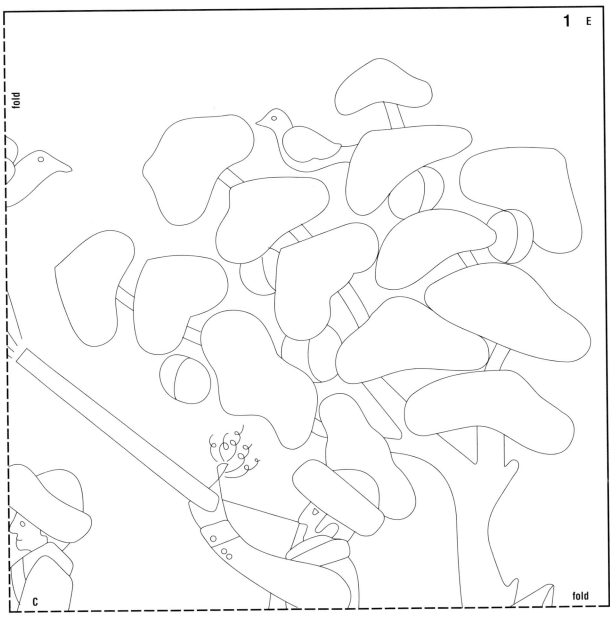

PATTERN #16: "Waterfowling"*

(Second page)

in these quilts, as well. To this day, duck blinds dot Maryland waterways and fowling is still enjoyed. But in the Victorian Album Quilt era, men hunting might also be seen as studying natural history and thus pursuing an edifying rational pleasure. The sport was useful in that it provided fresh victuals, but it also contained elements of instruction and moral uplift in that it took one into the great outdoors to marvel at God's plan.

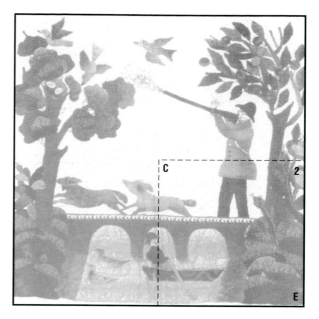

PATTERN #16: "Waterfowling"*

(Third page)

PATTERN #16: "Waterfowling"*

(Fourth page)

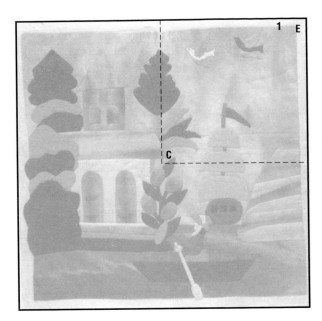

PATTERN #17: "Tropical Boating"*

Type: Baltimore-style
To make this block, refer to *Volume I*, Lesson 5 or 10. See also *Baltimore Album Quilts — Historic Notes and Antique Patterns*, Appendix I.

Reminiscent of a classic quilt block, the scene here seems greened by tropical foliage and quite exotic. A pagoda-like building and anchored clipper ship in the background bespeak far-off places. Yet the woman boating before us could be Baltimorean, perhaps a Victorian missionary's wife? She, or someone quite similar, may be seen at home rowing near a bridge where hunters pass by in yet another classic Album Quilt scene in Photo 4-17. Donna Collins, working in 1988, did a splendid job of using tie-dyed fabrics from New York Beauty to recreate the evocative old rainbow fabric effect of depth and contour.

PATTERN #17: "Tropical Boating"*

(Second page)

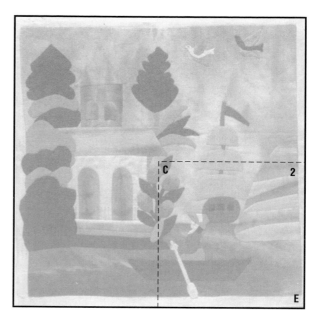

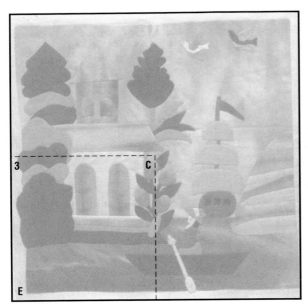

PATTERN #17: "Tropical Boating"*

(Third page)

PATTERN #17: "Tropical Boating"*

(Fourth page)

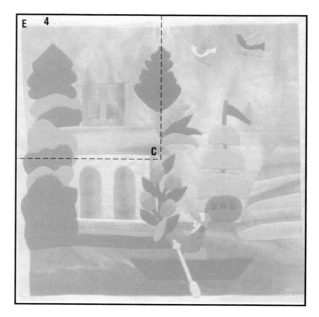

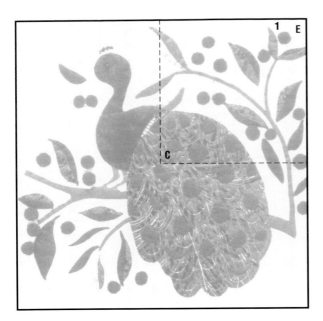

PATTERN #18: "Joy Nichol's Peacock"*

Type: "Beyond" Baltimore
To make this block, refer to *Volume I, Lesson 10*. See also
Baltimore Album Quilts — Historic Notes and Antique Patterns,
Appendix I.

The exotic, magnificently decorative peacock was a favorite
tropical bird for inclusion in one's Album Quilt. Joy Nichols designed this elegant pattern. She presents it splendidly here out of
an evocative print with the tail feathers stem-stitch outlined in
gold thread and their "eyes" fashioned of applied purple circles.
The bird's eye is a bright black button bead which echoes the
dimensionality of the stuffed cherries.

There is a possibility that peacocks were so common in the
classic Album Quilts for symbolic reasons as well as aesthetic
ones. Legend held that the peacock's body does not decay, making of them a visible sign of the concept of immortality. And this,
of course is what symbols do — provide a visible sign of something that is invisible. In Christian iconography, too, the hundred
tail-feather eyes symbolize the All-Seeing Eye of the Church and
of God. The All-Seeing Eye of God was an important precept of

PATTERN #18: "Joy Nichol's Peacock"*

(Second page)

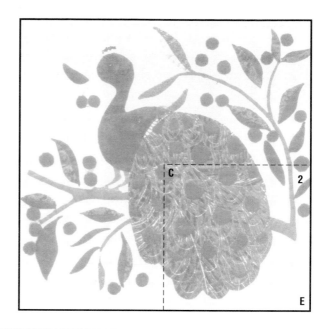

the Freemasons and the Odd Fellows whose symbolism so permeates many of these quilts. And thus one cannot dismiss the possibility that where the All-Seeing Eye of God is represented, it might have fraternal order connotations. Stuff of the spirit seems to have been so important to the Victorian quiltmakers: friendship, truth, remembrance, devotion, loyalty, charity, divine music, immortality, religion, patriotism, glory, duty, honor, country, courage, faith, hope, love, benevolence, sweet character, good deeds…. Perhaps these symbols and the stuff of the spirit they represent connect us to these quilts more powerfully than we care to admit or can even understand.

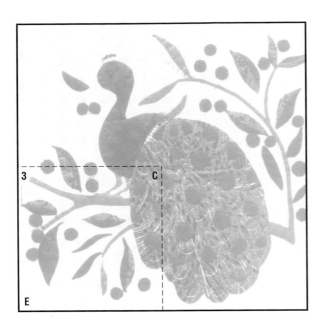

PATTERN #18: "Joy Nichol's Peacock"*

(Third page)

PATTERN #18: "Joy Nichol's Peacock"*

(Fourth page)

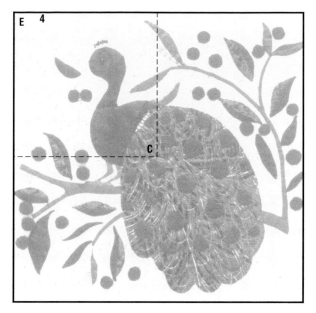

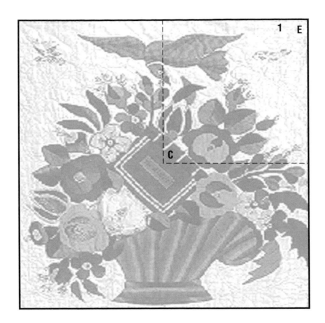

PATTERN #19: "Updegraf Basket, Book, and Bird"*

Type: Classic Baltimore
To make this block, refer to *Volume I*, Lesson 10. See also *Baltimore Album Quilts — Historic Notes and Antique Patterns*, Appendix I.

Baskets, books, birds — classic themes in classic quilts. Seemingly most often labeled Bible or Holy Bible, some books are simply labeled, as is this one, "Album." And so we come back to the Album. But now one's sense of the Album and its importance to the Victorians has caught our attention, connected us to them. And that, it seems, is what Album Quilts did and do — affirm, remember, "connect." At their best, Album Quilts were artfully presented collections that pushed the limits of variations on a theme. This block's designer must have been particularly pleased to extend the variety of Album presentations to this one where the book is presented gifted in a bouquet, an album itself within an Album!

PATTERN #19: "Updegraf Basket, Book, and Bird"*

(Second page)

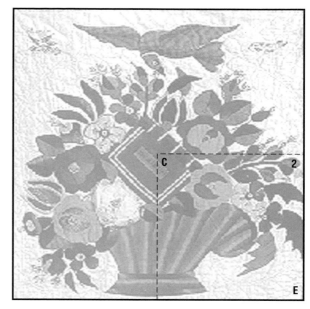

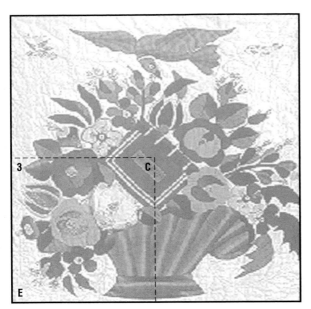

PATTERN #19: **"Updegraf Basket, Book, and Bird"***

(Third page)

PATTERN #19: "Updegraf Basket, Book, and Bird"*

(Fourth page)

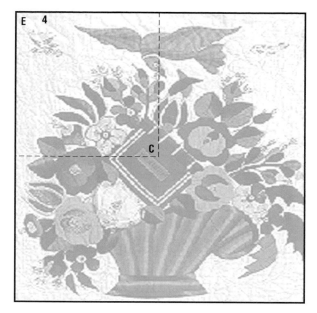

PATTERN #20: "Jeanne's Grapevine Wreath"*

Type: "Beyond" Baltimore
To make this block, refer to *Volume I*, Lessons 9 and 10. See also *Baltimore Album Quilts — Historic Notes and Antique Patterns*, Appendix I.

Jeanne Benson designed this winning block for the 1984 contest based on *Spoken Without a Word*. While it is entirely of her own design, the Victorian quiltmakers would undoubtedly have loved it. For it has characteristics they seem so to have admired: a balanced asymmetry, an airiness to the pattern, a pleasing naturalism to the stylization, and what appears to have been their very favorite Album Quilt fruit, the grapevine. Jeanne's soft, subtle colors work well with the brighter ones in *Volume I*'s quilt #7, where this block appears.

PATTERN #20: "Jeanne's Grapevine Wreath"*

(Second page)

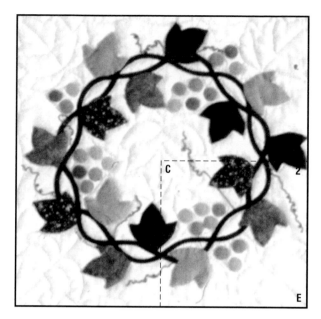

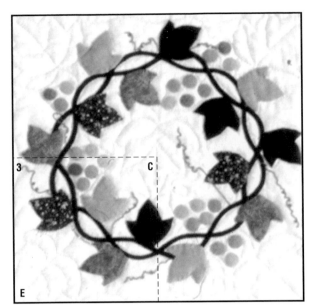

PATTERN #20: "Jeanne's Grapevine Wreath"*

(Third page)

PATTERN #20: "Jeanne's Grapevine Wreath"*

(Fourth page)

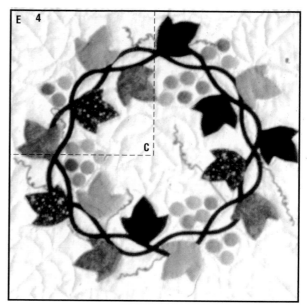

Borders

Thirteen borders are presented here, a beginning to the much greater offering of borders in the pattern companion to this volume. Three are classic borders sported by "beyond" Baltimore quilts (#6 and #7 in *Volume I*, and quilt #13 here in the Color Section). Patterns #21 and #24 through #33 are whole cloth or cutwork appliqué edging borders, many of which can also be seen on antique quilts pictured herein.

The favorite classic borders could be described as center-running borders and edging borders. In center-running borders, a contiguous motif is continuously repeated along the border's center length (as in a vine or in a swag border with connecting bow or flower). Edging borders decorate the border's outside edges with a contiguously repeated shape: scallops, a row of dogtooth triangles, steps, and so forth. The exciting thing about center-running borders and edging borders is that they are splendidly "mix-and-matchable." Where one quilt will have a simple dogtooth border edging with white space (dimensioned with quilting) in between, another will have a rose vine meandering between the serrate rows of edging.

Yet another will have the same vine, but with no appliquéd edging. See what mix-and-match combinations you recognize in the Gallery Quilts. There are lots of them — and both their similarities and their differences reinforce the mystery of Baltimore. Where did these women gather? How and by whom were templates drafted? How did they share ideas, patterns, fabrics? What design sources and design traditions influenced them? Who appliquéd what? What was going on? And why then, and why so often in Baltimore?

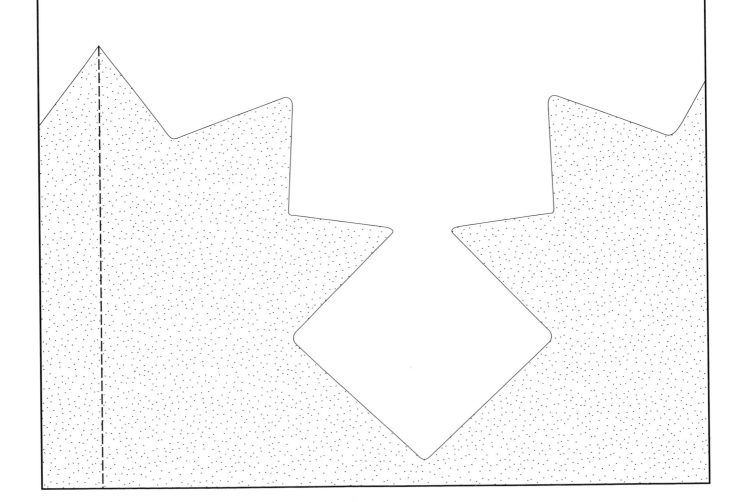

PATTERN #21: Peony Border (corner)

This line bisects the border's corner

This is the mid-line of the Peony Motif.

PATTERN #22: Peony and Hammock Border (2)

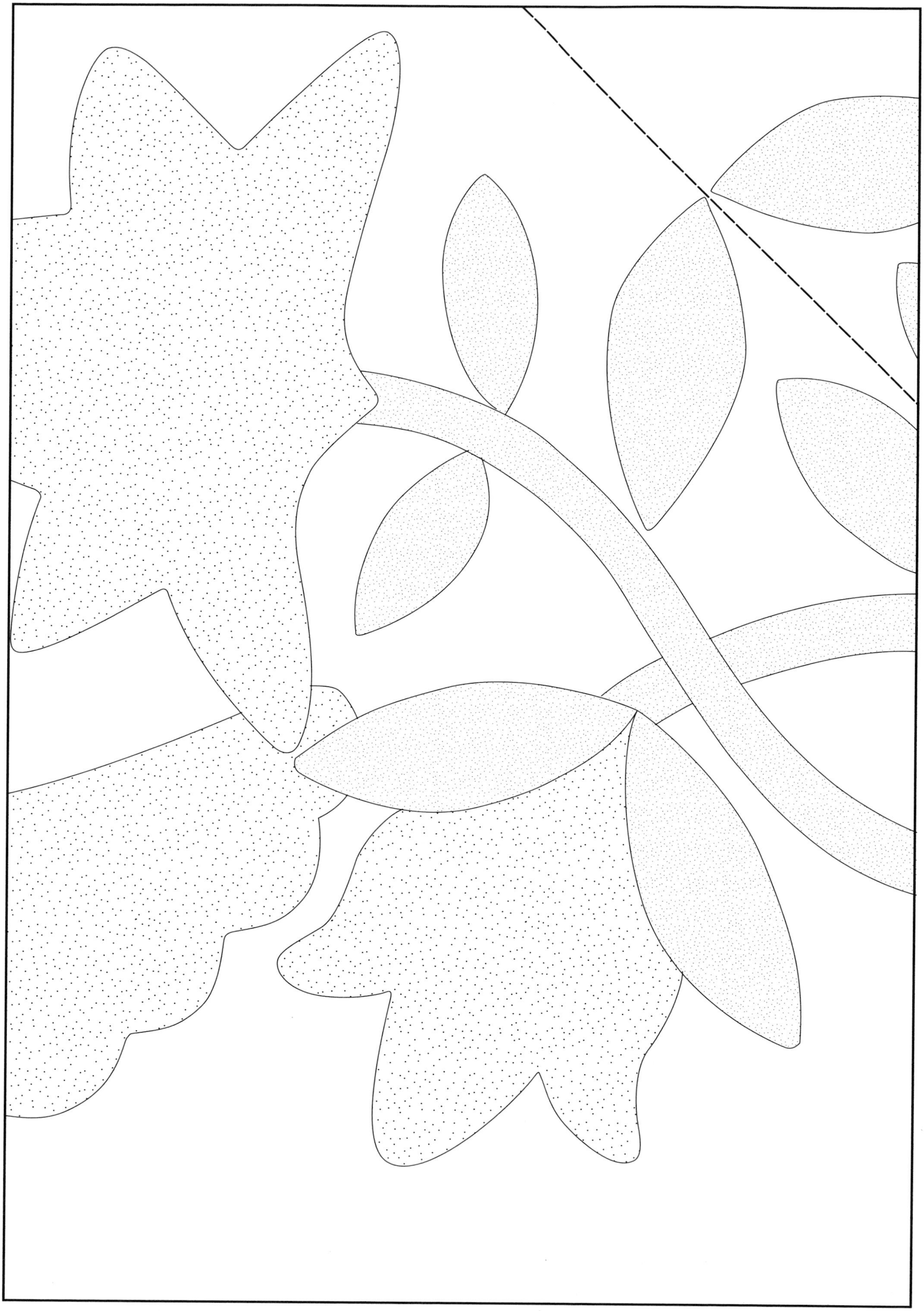

This line bisects the border's corner

PATTERN #23: Hammock and Bow Border (1)

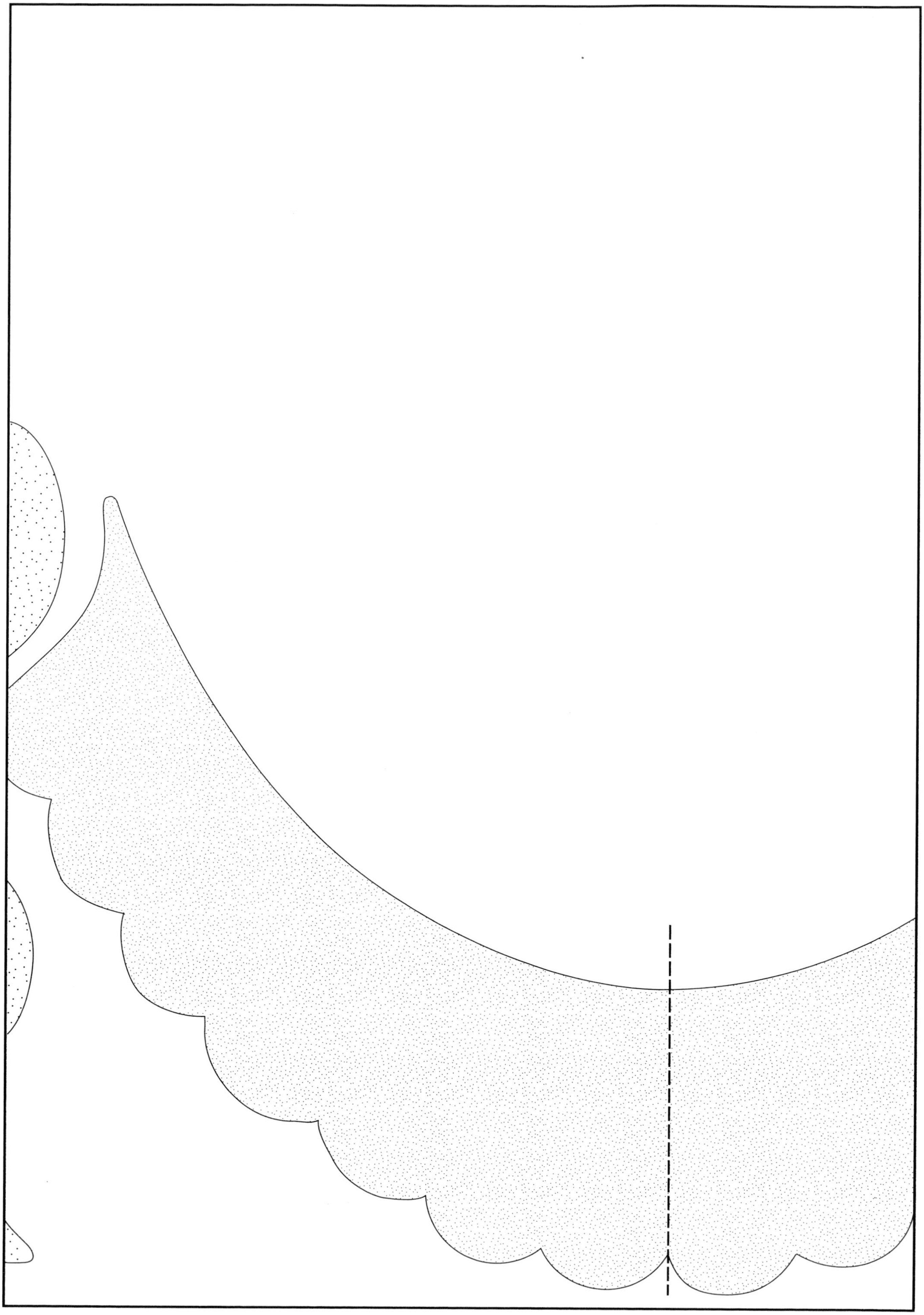

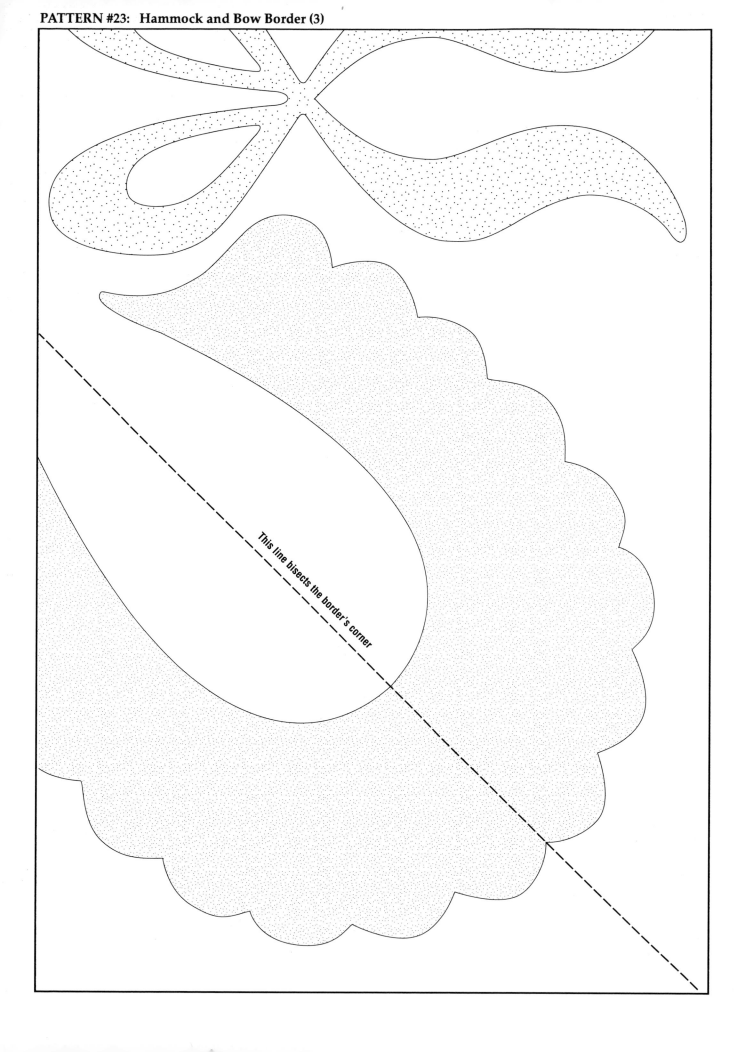

This line bisects the border's corner

PATTERN #24: Scalloped Border

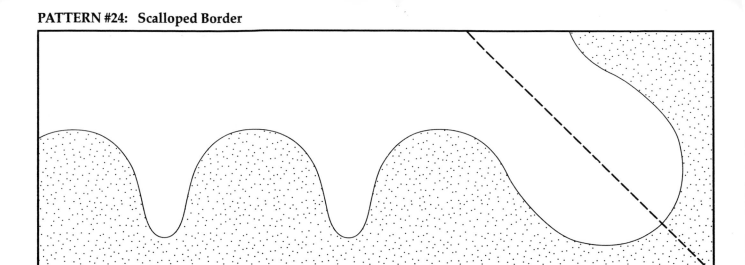

PATTERN #25: Stepped Border (four steps)

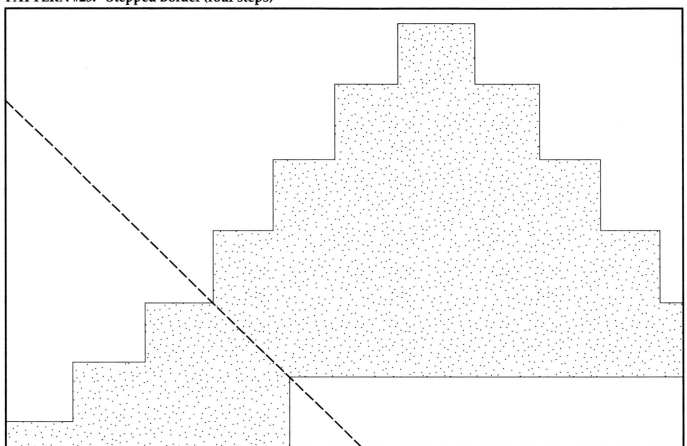

PATTERN #26: Dogtooth Border (of a size to be used alone)

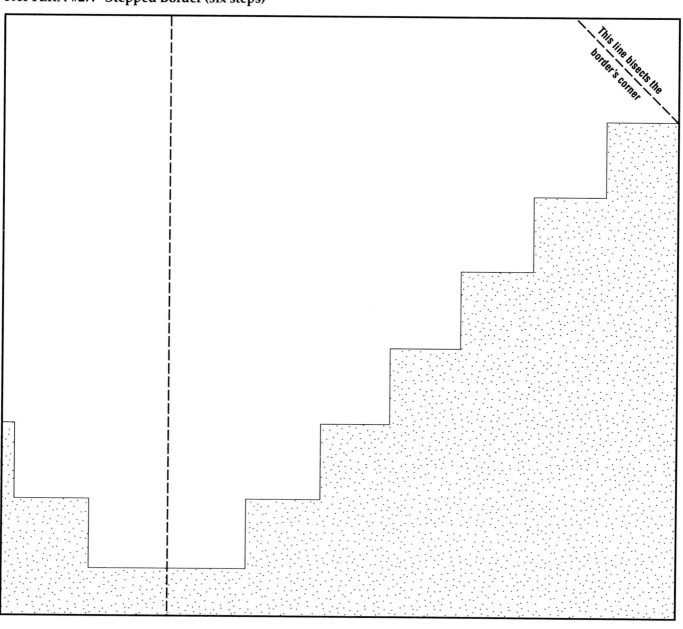

PATTERN #27: Stepped Border (six steps)

This line bisects the border's corner

PATTERN #28: Ruffled Border

This line bisects the border's corner

PATTERN #29: Dogtooth Triangle Border I

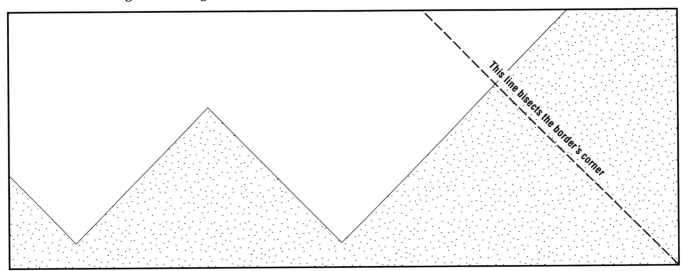

This line bisects the border's corner

PATTERN #30: Dogtooth Triangle Border II

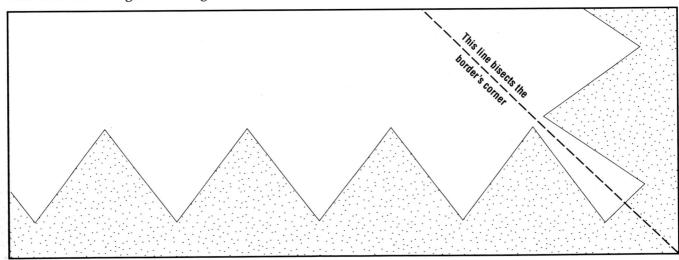

This line bisects the border's corner

PATTERN #31: Scalloped Border (of a size to be used alone)

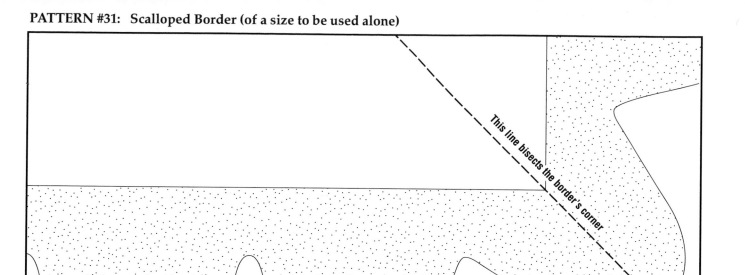

This line bisects the border's corner

PATTERN #32: Stepped Border (three steps)

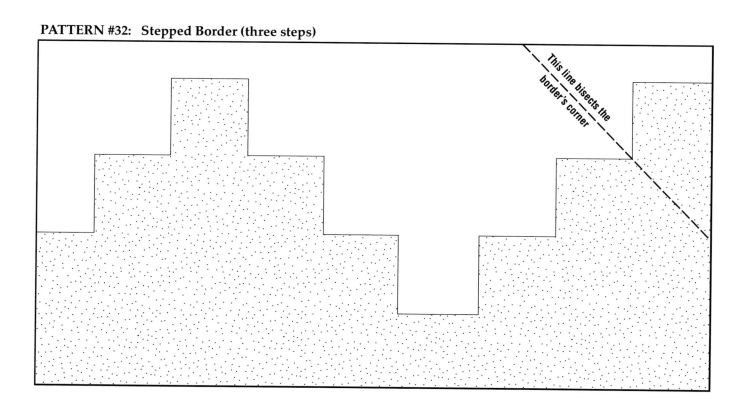

This line bisects the border's corner

PATTERN #33:   Canopy of Heaven Border

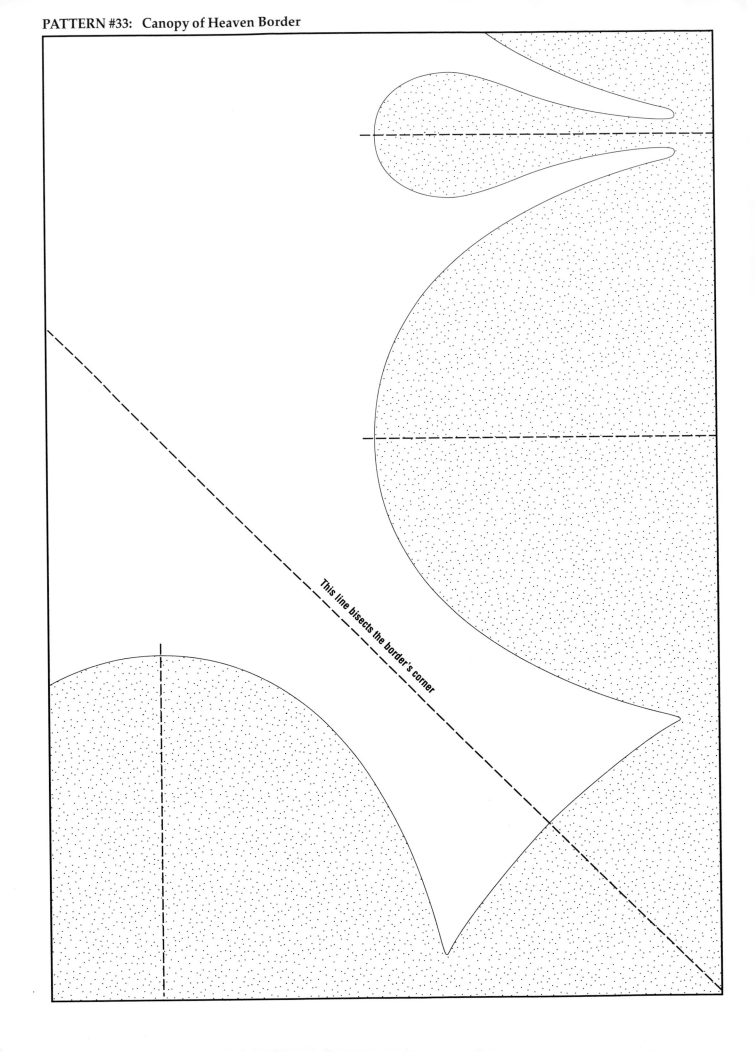

This line bisects the border's corner

Bibliography

History and Design Background

Barber, Lynn. *The Heyday of Natural History*. Doubleday, New York, 1980.

Beirne, Francis. *The Amiable Baltimoreans*. Johns Hopkins University Press, Baltimore, Md., 1984.

Bickham, George. *The Universal Penman*. (Originally published by George Bickham, London, circa 1740-41.) Dover, New York, 1954.

Bordes, Marilyn. *Twelve Great Quilts from the American Wing*. Metropolitan Museum of Art, New York, 1974.

Brackman, Barbara. "Buds and Blossoms: Nineteenth-Century Album Patterns." *Quilter's Newsletter Magazine*, #213, June 1989, pp. 24-26.

Brown, Becky. "A Shared Treasure: The Penn-Magruder Family Baltimore Album Quilt." *American Quilter*, Summer 1988, pp. 12-13.

Caulfeild, Sophia Frances Anne, and Saward, Blanche. *Encyclopedia of Victorian Needlework, Volumes I and II*. (Originally published in 1882 as *The Dictionary of Needlework: An Encyclopedia of Artistic, Plain, and Fancy Needlework*.) Dover, New York, 1972.

Chittenden, Fred J., editor. *The Royal Horticultural Society Dictionary of Gardening, A Practical and Scientific Encyclopaedia of Horticulture*. Second edition. Clarendon Press, Oxford, 1956; corrected and reprinted, 1965.

Colby, Averil. *Patchwork*. B. T. Botsford, Ltd., London, 1973.

Cunz, D. *The Maryland Germans, A History*. Princeton University Press, Princeton, N.J., 1948.

Dunton, William Rush, Jr. *Notebooks* (unpublished). In the Baltimore Museum of Art, Baltimore, Md.

Dunton, William Rush, Jr. *Old Quilts*. Published by the author, Catonsville, Md., 1946.

Federal Writers' Project, Works Progress Administration. *Washington, D.C.: A Guide to the Nation's Capital*. Hastings House, New York, 1942.

Ferrero, Pat, Hedges, Elaine, and Silber, Julie. *Hearts and Hands: The Influence of Women and Quilts in American Society*. Quilt Digest Press, San Francisco, 1987.

Finley, Ruth. *Old Patchwork Quilts and the Women Who Made Them*. Lippincott, Philadelphia, 1929; reprinted by C. T. Branford Company, Newton Centre, Mass.,1983.

Gillon, Edmund V., Jr., editor. *Cartouches and Decorative Small Frames*. Dover Publications, New York, 1975.

Grafton, Carol Belanger, editor. *1001 Floral Motifs and Ornaments for Artists and Crafts-people*. Dover Publications, New York, 1987.

_____. *Pictorial Archives of Decorative Frames and Labels: 550 Copyright-Free Designs*. Dover Publications, New York, 1982.

Hillstrom, Judith. "The Christmas Cactus." *American Horticulture Magazine*, Dec. 1988, pp. 38-40.

Jenkins, Reese V. *Images and Enterprise: Technology and the American Photographic Industry, 1839-1925*. Johns Hopkins University Press, Baltimore, Md., 1975.

Jones, Owen. *The Grammar of Ornament: All 100 Color Plates from the Folio Edition of the Great Victorian Scrapbook of Historic Design*. (First published in England, 1856.) Portland House, New York, 1986.

Katzenberg, Dena. *Baltimore Album Quilts*. Baltimore Museum of Art, Baltimore, Md., 1981.

Laury, Jean Ray, and The California Heritage Quilt Project. *Ho For California*. Dutton, New York, 1990.

Lavitt, Wendy, and Weissman, Judith Reiter. *Labors of Love: America's Textiles and Needlework, 1650-1930*. Knopf, New York, 1987.

McKelvey, Susan. *Friendship's Offering: Techniques and Inspirations for Writing on Quilts*. C & T Publishing, Lafayette, Calif., 1990.

McSherry, James. *History of Maryland*. Baltimore Book Company, Baltimore, Md., 1904.

Nelson, Cyril, editor. *The Quilt Engagement Calendar*. Dutton, New York, 1983, 1984, 1985, 1987, 1988.

Nicoll, Jessica F. *Quilted for Friends*. Henry Francis Du Pont Winterthur Museum, Winterthur, Delaware, 1986.

Orlofsky, Patsy and Myron. *Quilts in America*. McGraw-Hill, New York, 1974.

Peto, Florence. *Historic Quilts*. American Historical Company, New York, 1939.

Rae, Janet. *The Quilts of the British Isles*. Dutton, New York, 1987.

Ring, Betty. *American Needlework Treasures, Samples, and Silk Embroideries from the Collection of Betty Ring*. Dutton, New York, 1987.

Rumford, Beatrix T., and Weekley, Carolyn J. *Treasures of American Folk Art: from the Abby Aldrich Rockefeller Folk Art Center*. Little, Brown, Boston, 1989.

Schlesinger, Arthur M., Jr., editor. *The Almanac of American History*. Putnam, New York, 1983.

Sienkiewicz, Elly. "Album Quilts and Victorian Inkings." *Traditional Quiltworks*, February/March/April 1989, pp. 27-34.

_____. "Baltimore Album Quilts," *Quilts Japan No. 14*. Nihon Vogue Company Limited, Tokyo, Japan, 1990, pp. 59-74.

_____. *Baltimore Album Quilts — Historic Notes and Antique Patterns, A Pattern Companion to Baltimore Beauties and Beyond, Volume I*. C & T Publishing, Lafayette, Calif., 1990.

_____. *Baltimore Beauties and Beyond: Studies in Classic Album Quilt Appliqué, Volume I*. C & T Publishing, Lafayette, Calif., 1989.

_____. "Friendship's Offering." *Quilter's Newsletter Magazine*, #212, May 1989, pp. 32-37.

_____. "My Baltimore Album Quilt Discoveries." *Quilter's Newsletter Magazine*, #202, May 1988, pp. 26-27.

_____. "The Numsen Quilt: Fancy Flowers from Old Baltimore." *Quilter's Newsletter Magazine*, #218, January 1990, pp. 12-15.

_____. *Spoken Without a Word: A Lexicon of Selected Symbols with 24 Patterns from Classic Baltimore Album Quilts*. Published by the author, Washington, D.C., 1983.

_____. "Victorian Album Quilts." *Quilter's Newsletter Magazine*, #217, November/December 1989, pp. 32-34, 70.

_____."The World's Most Valuable Quilt." *Quilting Today*, #12, April, May 1989, pp. 6-7, 48.

Sotheby's, Inc. *Important Americana [catalogue], Sale #5680, January 1988.* Sotheby's, New York, 1987.

Spencer, Richard Henry, editor. *Genealogical and Memorial Encyclopedia of the State of Maryland. A Record of the Achievement of Her People in the Making of a Commonwealth and the Founding of a Nation.* American Historical Society, New York, 1919.

Titus, Charles. *The Old Line State: Her Heritage.* Tidewater Publishers, Cambridge, Md., 1971.

The United States Capitol Historical Society. *Washington Past and Present, A Guide to the Nation's Capital.* The United States Capitol Historical Society, Washington, D.C., 1983.

_____. *We, The People: The Story of the United States Capitol.* The United States Capitol Historical Society, Washington, D.C., 1964.

Victorian Frames, Borders, and Cuts. Dover Publications, New York, 1976.

Von Gwinner, Schnuppe. *The History of the Patchwork Quilt: Origins, Traditions, and Symbols of a Textile Art.* Keyser Book Publishing, Munich, Germany, 1987.

Warren, Mame and Marion E. *Maryland Time Exposures, 1840-1940.* Johns Hopkins University Press, Baltimore, Md., 1984.

Wright, Roxa. "Baltimore Friendship Quilt." *Woman's Day,* October 1965.

Zaner-Bloser, Inc. *The Zanerian Manual of Alphabets and Engrossing.* Zaner-Bloser, Columbus, Ohio, 1981.

Symbolism, and Symbolism in the Classic Album Quilts

Barth, Edna. *Hearts, Cupids, and Red Roses: The Story of the Valentine Symbols.* Seabury Press, New York, 1974.

_____. *Holly, Reindeer, and Colored Lights: The Story of the Christmas Symbols.* Seabury Press, New York, 1971.

_____. *Lilies, Rabbits, and Painted Eggs: The Story of the Easter Symbols.* Seabury Press, New York, 1970.

_____. *Shamrocks, Harps, and Shillelaghs: The Story of the St. Patrick's Day Symbols.* Seabury Press, New York, 1977.

_____. *Turkeys, Pilgrims, and Indian Corn: The Story of the Thanksgiving Symbols.* Seabury Press, New York, 1975.

_____. *Witches, Pumpkins, and Grinning Ghosts: The Story of the Halloween Symbols.* Seabury Press, New York, 1974.

Beharrell, Thomas G. *Odd Fellows Monitor and Guide, Containing History of the Degree of Rebekah, and Its Teachings, Emblems of the Order, According to Present Classification, and Teachings of Ritual, As Understood by Obligated Odd Fellows and their Wives, With A Brief History of Our Examples, In Three Parts.* Robert Douglass, Indianapolis, 1878.

Cirlot, Juan Eduardo. *A Dictionary of Symbols.* Translated by Jack Sage. Philosophical Library, New York, 1962.

Cross, Jeremy L. *The True Masonic Chart or Hieroglyphic Monitor Containing All the Emblems Explained in the Degrees of Entered Apprentice, Fellow Craft, Master Mason, Mark Master, Past Master, Most Excellent Master, Royal Arch, Royal Master, and Select Master.* Engraved and Printed for the Author, New Haven, 1824.

Ferguson, George. *Signs & Symbols in Christian Art.* Oxford University Press, New York, 1954.

Franco, Barbara. *Masonic Symbolism in American Decorative Arts.* Scottish Rite Masonic Museum and Library, Lexington, Mass., 1976.

_____. *Fraternally Yours.* Scottish Rite Masonic Museum and Library, Lexington, Mass., 1986.

Peroni, Laura. *The Language of Flowers.* Crown, New York, 1982.

Sienkiewicz, Elly. *Spoken Without a Word: A Lexicon of Selected Symbols with 24 Patterns from Classic Baltimore Album Quilts.* Published by the author, Washington, D.C., 1983.

Spencer, F. *Chrismons, An Explanation of the Symbols on the Chrismons Tree at the Ascension Lutheran Church in Danville, Virginia.* Womack Press, Danville, Va., 1970.

Pictures of Appliquéd Album Quilts

Allen, Gloria Seaman. *Old Line Traditions, Maryland Women and Their Quilts.* DAR Museum, Washington, D.C., 1985.

Bacon, Lenice Ingram. *American Patchwork Quilts.* Morrow, New York, 1973.

Bank, Mirra, compiler. *Anonymous Was a Woman.* St. Martin's Press, New York, 1979.

Bath, Virginia. *Needlework in America: History, Designs, and Techniques.* Viking Press, New York, 1979.

Betterton, Shiela. *Quilts and Coverlets from the American Museum in Britain.* Butler & Tanner, London, 1978, 1982.

Bishop, Robert. *The Knopf Collectors' Guides to American Antiques.* Knopf, New York, 1982.

_____. *New Discoveries in American Quilts.* Dutton, New York, 1975.

Bullard, Lacy Folmar, and Shiell, Betty Jo. *Chintz Quilts: Unfading Glory.* Serendipity Publishers, Tallahassee, Fla., 1983.

Fox, Sandi. *Small Endearments: Nineteenth-Century Quilts for Children.* Scribner, New York, 1985.

Hinson, Dolores. *American Graphic Quilt Designs.* Arco, New York, 1983.

Houck, Carter, and Nelson, Cyril. *The Quilt Engagement Calendar Treasury.* Dutton, New York, 1982.

Katzenberg, Dena. *Baltimore Album Quilts.* Baltimore Museum of Art, Baltimore, Md., 1981.

Kolter, Jane Bentley. *Forget Me Not: A Gallery of Friendship and Album Quilts.* Main Street Press, Pittstown, N.J., 1985.

Lasansky, Jeannette. *In the Heart of Pennsylvania.* Oral Traditions Project of the Union County Historical Society, Lewisburg, Pa., 1985.

_____. *In the Heart of Pennsylvania, Symposium Papers.* Oral Traditions Project of the Union County Historical Society, Lewisburg, Pa., 1986.

_____. *Pieced by Mother: Over One Hundred Years of Quiltmaking Traditions.* The Oral Traditions Project of the Union County Historical Society, Lewisburg, Pa., 1987.

Lipman, Jean, and Winchester, Alice. *The Flowering of American Folk Art, 1776-1876.* Running Press, Philadelphia, Pa., 1974.

Orlofsky, Patsy and Myron. *Quilts in America.* McGraw-Hill, New York, 1974.

Quilt Digest. Numbers 1 and 2. Kiracofe and Kile, San Francisco, 1983, 1984.

Quilt Digest. Numbers 3, 4, and 5. Quilt Digest Press, San Francisco, 1987.

Rumford, Beatrix T., and Weekley, Carolyn J. *Treasures of American Folk Art: from the Abby Aldrich Rockefeller Folk Art Center,* Little, Brown, Boston, 1989.

Safford, Carleton, and Bishop, Robert. *America's Quilts and Coverlets.* Weathervane Books/Dutton, New York, 1972.

Smyth, Frances P., and Yakush, Mary, editors. *An American Sampler: Folk Art from the Shelburne Museum.* National Gallery of Art, Washington, D.C., 1987.

Ungerleider-Mayerson, Joy. *Jewish Folk Art from Biblical Days to Modern Times.* Summit Books, New York, 1986.

Woodward, Thomas, and Greenstein, Blanche. *Crib Quilts and Other Small Wonders.* Dutton, New York, 1981.

Baltimore Album Quilt Patterns and Appliqué How-to

Boyink, Betty. *Flower Gardens and Hexagons for Quilters.* Published by the author, Grand Haven, Mich., 1984.

Hinson, Dolores. *American Graphic Quilt Designs.* Arco, New York, 1983.

Patera, Charlotte. *Cutwork Appliqué.* New Century, Pittstown, N.J., 1983.

Sienkiewicz, Elly. *Spoken Without a Word: A Lexicon of Selected Symbols with 24 Patterns from Classic Baltimore Album Quilts.* Published by the author, Washington, D.C., 1983.

_____. *Baltimore Album Quilts — Historic Notes and Antique Patterns, A Pattern Companion to Baltimore Beauties and Beyond, Volume I.* C & T Publishing, Lafayette, Calif., 1990.

_____. *Baltimore Beauties and Beyond: Studies in Classic Album Quilt Appliqué, Volume I.* C & T Publishing, Lafayette, Calif., 1989.

Appendix: Sources

If, after checking with your local quilt shop, you are still looking for a special service or supply, this brief listing may help.

Betty Boyink, 818 Sheldon Road, Grand Haven, MI 49417.
  Twenty-four-sheet tablet of 12" graph paper ideal for designing 12 ½" Album Quilt blocks. For ordering information, send SASE.

C & T Publishing, P.O. Box 1456, Lafayette, CA 94549. Phone (800) 284-1114.
  Baltimore Beauties and Beyond, Studies in Classic Album Quilt Appliqué, Volume I by Elly Sienkiewicz, $23.95 softbound; $34.95 hardbound. *Baltimore Album Quilts — Historic Notes and Antique Patterns, A Pattern Companion to Baltimore Beauties and Beyond, Volume I,* $23.95 softbound; $34.95 hardbound. Add $2.00 shipping for each volume.

The Cotton Patch, 1025 Brown Avenue, Lafayette, CA 94549.
  A good source for English needles: #10 or #11 Sharps or Milliners Needles. Sophisticated prints and background fabrics are included in The Cotton Patch's 300 swatches for $3.00. An extensive mail-order catalog, including information on Elly Sienkiewicz's *Baltimore Beauties* series, is free.

Empty Spools, Diana McClune, 70 Bradley Avenue, Walnut Creek, CA 94596.
  Pattern for quilt #14 in the Color Section, fully drafted by Adele Ingraham. The quilt is based on a 16" block. $50, plus $2.50 shipping.

New York Beauty Fabric and Design, Edith Tanniru, 610 Hamilton Parkway, Dewitt, NY 13214.
  Hand-dyed fabrics in shaded sets and tie-dyed fabrics as were used in quilt #15, "Petite Baltimore Album." For ordering information, send SASE.

The Quilted Apple, 2320 East Osborne Road, Phoenix, AZ 85016.
  Send a SASE for information on an Album Quilt pattern set such as quilt #3.

Judy Severson, 2935B Kerner, San Rafael, CA 94901.
  Judy's printmaking business offers embossed prints and elegant stationery for all occasions. Judy embosses quilting patterns upon the silk-screened quilt designs. Quilters will appreciate her exceptional talent for combining quilting with appliqué. For ordering information, send large SASE.

Elly Sienkiewicz, 5540 30th Street N.W., Washington, D.C. 20015.
  Spoken Without a Word: A Lexicon of Selected Symbols with 24 Patterns from Classic Baltimore Album Quilts, $18.95 plus $3.00 postage.

Christine Wellman, P.O. Box 863, Georgetown, MA 01833.
  Elegant hand-marbleized cottons. For ordering information, send SASE.

Zaner-Bloser, 612 North Park Street, Columbus, OH 43215. Phone (614) 486-0221.
  Call or write for ordering information on *The Zanerian Manual of Alphabets and Engrossing.* A classic reference, this is probably the most thorough, reasonably priced manual on calligraphy in print.

About the Author and the Baltimore Beauties Series

 A quiltmaker for some sixteen years now, Elly Sienkiewicz has — since 1983 — been fascinated by the Baltimore-style Album Quilts. In that year, her first book on the subject, *Spoken Without a Word: A Lexicon of Selected Symbols with 24 Patterns from Classic Baltimore Album Quilts*, was self-published. Winners of a contest based on that book became latter-day "Ladies of Baltimore." The group has since grown. With their help, Elly has produced several appliqué Album Quilts shown in these volumes. She draws upon over two dozen years of teaching experience in writing the *Baltimore Beauties* series, published by C & T Publishing.

Baltimore Beauties and Beyond — Studies in Classic Album Quilt Appliqué, Volume I begins the series and teaches the intricacies of appliqué techniques in the context of these classic quilts. To its patterns for twenty-nine blocks, the sequel — *Baltimore Album Quilts — Historic Notes and Antique Patterns, A Pattern Companion to Volume I* — adds patterns for another fifty-eight blocks. The *Baltimore Beauties* series will include a pattern companion to *Volume II* featuring additional border patterns and fancy flower techniques, and *Volume III* which will focus on paper-cut or *scherenschnitte* Album quilts.

A teacher of secondary school history for seven years, Elly graduated from Wellesley College with a history major and art and religion minors. She received an M.S. Ed. from the University of Pennsylvania and finds her abiding interests well met in the study of these classic Album Quilts.

About the back cover

The block, on which is written "Queen of May," is a detail from the Baltimore-style Album Quilt, quilt #10 in the Color Section. The block "Waterfowling" is from that same quilt. A slightly different version of this block is given in Pattern #19. (Photos courtesy of Hirschl & Adler Folk, NYC)

Other fine quilting books from C & T Publishing

An Amish Adventure, Roberta Horton
Baltimore Album Quilts — Historic Notes and Antique Patterns, Elly Sienkiewicz
Baltimore Beauties and Beyond, Volume I, Elly Sienkiewicz
Boston Commons Quilt, Blanche Young and Helen Young Frost
Calico and Beyond, Roberta Horton
A Celebration of Hearts, Jean Wells and Marina Anderson
Crazy Quilt Handbook, Judith Montano
Crazy Quilt Odyssey, Judith Montano
Crosspatch, Pepper Cory
Diamond Patchwork, Jeffrey Gutcheon
Fans, Jean Wells
Fine Feathers, Marianne Fons
Flying Geese Quilt, Blanche Young and Helen Young Frost
Friendship's Offering, Susan McKelvey
Heirloom Machine Quilting, Harriet Hargrave
Irish Chain Quilt, Blanche Young and Helen Young Frost
Landscapes and Illustions, Joel Wolfrom
Let's Make Waves, Marianne Fons and Liz Porter
Light and Shadows, Susan McKelvey
Mandala, Katie Pasquini
Mariner's Compass, Judy Mathieson
New Lone Star Handbook, Blanche Young and Helen Young Frost
Perfect Pineapples, Jane Hall and Dixie Haywood
Picture This, Jean Wells and Marina Anderson
Plaids and Stripes, Roberta Horton
Quilting Designs from the Amish, Pepper Cory
Quilting Designs from Antique Quilts, Pepper Cory
Radiant Nine Patch, Blanche Young
Stained Glass Quilting Technique, Roberta Horton
Trip Around the World Quilts, Blanche Young and Helen Young Frost
Visions: Quilts of a New Decade, Quilt San Diego
Working in Miniature, Becky Schaefer
Wearable Art for Real People, Mary Mashuta
3 Dimensional Design, Katie Pasquini

For more information, write for a free catalog from:
C & T Publishing
P.O. Box 1456
Lafayette, CA 94549

This is the end of Volume Two.